ARCHITECTURAL DRAWING AND DRAUGHTSMEN

British Library Cataloguing-in-Publication Data
A catalogue record for this book is available from the
British Library

Raising the Great Obelisk of the Vatican: "The Guglia." From *Della Trasportazione dell' Obelisco Vaticano* (p. 18). By Domenico Fontana.

ARCHITECTURAL DRAWING · AND DRAUGHTSMEN

By REGINALD BLOMFIELD, A.R.A.

WITH ONE HUNDRED AND THREE ILLUSTRATIONS

PREFACE

THE following account of architectural drawing and draughtsmen is intended mainly for students, and its object is to show that architectural draughtsmanship is not cut off from the family of Art, but that, in the hands of artists of genius, it has gone far, and takes a higher place than has usually been assigned it by artists and critics. As a matter of fact, not very much attention has been paid to this subject in England. William Burges read a paper on architectural drawing at the Royal Institute of British Architects in 1860; an excellent and well-illustrated paper was given there by Mr. Maurice B. Adams in 1885; and a book on architectural drawing, by Mr. R. Phené Spiers, himself an admirable draughtsman, appeared in 1887. Mr. Adams's paper is valuable for its account of English architectural draughtsmen of the last century; Mr. Spiers's book for its very useful hints on the *mécanique* of drawing.

The standpoint from which the present work is written is different. I have endeavoured to extend the conception of draughtsmanship by including in my survey French and Italian draughtsmen, some of whom are very little known or studied in England, and incidentally to widen its range by including men who were designers almost as much as draughtsmen, such as the Lepautre, the Marot, and the French draughtsmen of the seventeenth and eighteenth centuries. The tendency of students is to concentrate on the favourite manner of the time, and neglect any other. This is not the way to become a fine draughtsman, and the illustrations that I have brought together are intended to correct

Preface

this tendency, by showing that there is no royal road to draughtsmanship. The basis of it must be the study of form, and its mastery ; and its final expression must be fine drawing, inspired by personal temperament. I should add that my account in no sense claims to be exhaustive, and I need hardly point out to students that though I have, of necessity, laid stress on draughtsmanship, the object of their training is not the production of a brilliant drawing at our annual exhibitions, but the finer and far more difficult task of designing noble architecture.

I must express my obligations to the Keeper of the Prints and Drawings in the British Museum, to the Librarian of the Royal Institute of British Architects (Mr. Dircks), to the Warden and Fellows of All Souls' College, the Provost and Fellows of Worcester College, Oxford, and to the Trustees and the Curator of the Soane Museum (Mr. Walter Spiers), for their courteous permission to reproduce the drawings in their custody.

REGINALD BLOMFIELD.

NEW COURT, TEMPLE,
September, 1912

CONTENTS

LIST OF ILLUSTRATIONS

x   List of Illustrations

ARCHITECTURAL DRAWING AND DRAUGHTSMEN

CHAPTER I

THE NATURE AND PURPOSE OF ARCHITECTURAL DRAWING— MEDIEVAL DRAWINGS

ARCHITECTURAL draughtsmanship has fallen from the high place it once occupied, and has been cut off from the main stream of Art, and in the following chapters I hope, by reference to the past, to recover some of this lost territory, and to disentangle the ideals to be aimed at in such drawing, and the point of view from which it should be approached. To arrive at this result I do not intend to offer a technical disquisition on geometrical drawing, isometrical projection, perspective and skiography, essential as all these are in the student's training, but rather to enlarge the scope of our conception of architectural drawing by tracing its development in the past and by reviewing the work of certain great masters of the art, of men who have risen above the ranks of the mere technician, not only by their dexterity, but by rarer qualities of selection, insight, and imaginative power.

The tendency to concentrate attention on contemporary work, to the neglect of the study of the past, is peculiarly dangerous in the case of the Arts, because the standard of appreciation, the tests to be applied to the works of living artists, are apt to degenerate through simple ignorance of what has actually been done in the past ; and though, of course, students will note the work of their contemporaries, and indeed cannot help doing so, it

B

is not here that one should search for the touchstone of criticism, but in the achievements of men long since dead.

In this brief survey I do not include the work of living draughtsmen, excellent as many of them are, because it is not for artists to criticise the works of their professional brethren, and it is exceedingly difficult to judge fairly and accurately the work of men with whom we are brought into daily contact, and who in some cases enjoy more, and in some less, reputation than they are fairly entitled to. Fashion has so much to do with current reputations, that the only safe standard to judge by is that set by men who have long been recognised by competent judges as past masters of their art. For that, after all, is the only working test. Ingenious writers may find transcendent merit in the work of some long-forgotten artist, and in some rare instances the merit is genuine, particularly in the case of architects whose work is difficult to trace, and whom not only the public but artists are slow to recognise. But the verdict of time is seldom wholly wrong, and students, at any rate in their period of training, will be wise to take as their masters only those artists whose reputation has stood the test of time, and to regard with an open mind, and even suspend judgment on, methods and models that are still in the melting-pot.

It is always a difficult problem to assess contemporary progress. There is the danger of mistaking a fancy of the time for a genuine movement, and the scorn with which one may be tempted to regard the work of two or three generations back may recoil on one's own head. There was an example of this in the exhibition of the work of deceased masters at Burlington House a few years ago in the case of the late Mr. Frith. The attitude of art critics to the works of that artist was well known, but his picture of "Ramsgate Sands," a comparatively early work, exhibited a technique scarcely inferior to that of Hogarth himself. It was not that the critics were substantially wrong, but that their survey was incomplete. The verdict of time is lost sight of in the craze for the latest thing in Art, and this is one of the pitfalls that lie in wait for the student. The ease and rapidity with which ideas can be interchanged is actually a danger in the Arts. A hundred years ago and earlier there were fashions too, but they were fashions of considerable solidity, changing not year by year, but generation by generation, and the student in mastering the fashion of his generation at any rate mastered one manner fairly completely. Nowadays he is apt to dash from one manner to another, and never arrives at anything. It is essential that the student, in selecting his models for imitation, should fortify his judgment by the study of history and the analysis of old work.

A good deal of caution is wise in appreciating the progress of contemporary draughtsmanship. These brilliant water-colours, these audacious presentations of architecture that thrill the unwary in our modern exhibitions—are they really better than the drawings of fifty years ago? Or is it only their novelty and contempt for accepted traditions that seduce our judgment? Are our line and wash drawings up to the standard of Girtin? Is there any living draughtsman who can use his pen and his blot as Piranesi did in his improvisations, those lightning transcripts of his imagination? One has to admit that there are no such draughtsmen to-day. But, on the other hand, if one shifts the standard, if one compares modern drawing or modern architecture with what was accepted as such in England fifty years ago, I do not doubt that there is a marked improvement. In spite of much that is extravagant and even absurd, our modern architectural drawings are better than the laborious perspectives, the wiry and insensitive line, the absurd conventions, and the acrid colouring of the draughtsmen of the 'sixties and 'seventies. And the reason why I venture this assertion is that the fashionable architecture—and with it the draughtsmanship—of the middle of the nineteenth century was founded on no solid basis of inheritance ; it sprang out of nothing in history, and it has ended in nothing, except that, as a reaction against this unprofitable emptiness, artists have gone back to earlier traditions. In recent years they have attached themselves more particularly to the French tradition of draughtsmanship, which in the last twenty years has to some extent dominated this country and has taken complete possession of America. Fine as that tradition is, it is by no means the complete and only standard of architectural draughtsmanship ; far from it ; it is itself only a very dexterous convention which attains its perfection by eliminating half the problem. We must go much farther afield than this if we are to understand the whole gamut of notes on which a great architectural draughtsman can play.

That, however, is a point which will appear later, and we must start with a clear conception of the province and intention of architectural drawing and illustration, for the subject is a large one, and cannot be dealt with exclusively from one point of view. Generally, the object of architectural drawing is the representation of architecture. It will include a wide field of draughtsmanship, ranging from the plainest and most practical working drawing made for the purpose of actual building, to the opposite pole of such wild visions of architecture as Piranesi gave the world in his *Carcere d' Invenzione*. It will not include, for the purpose of this study, the architectural backgrounds of pictures, such as the courts of Carlo Crivelli, or the porticoes and terraces of Veronese. Architecture in these pictures is subordinate—it is there to help out another idea ; and though its presentation implies a knowledge of architectural form and composition, and powers of draughtsmanship in this regard, such as are seldom to be found in modern painting, the question here is in its main

Purpose of Architectural Drawing

issues a painter's question, to be determined by other considerations than those of the presentation of architecture; and I would only call the attention of all students in painting to the necessity for its serious study as an essential part of their training for decorative painting.

A difference at once presents itself in architectural drawings according to the intention with which they are made. This intention may be either objective or subjective; that is, the intention of the draughtsman may be either to make drawings which can be carried out in the building by other hands exactly as drawn, or, on the other hand, he may wish to produce in somebody else's mind the impression of the building as a whole as he conceives it, or he may employ architectural forms as the symbols and embodiments of some abstract idea, the imagery of a world which never has existed in fact, and never can. Some of the French draughtsmen so used them in the seventeenth century, and, in a far more notable manner, Piranesi in the eighteenth. In the first case he will proceed by geometrical drawings; in the second and third by perspective representation, with such accessories as skiography, figure or landscape drawing, and the like, as may be necessary to drive home his ideas.

The geometrical drawings are the usual plans, sections, and elevations of a design familiar to the architectural student, and generally set out to a scale of $\frac{1}{8}$ and $\frac{1}{4}$ inch to the foot. There are only two essential conditions of such drawings: (1) that they should be perfectly accurate; (2) that they should be perfectly clear. The first condition is, of course, largely one of knowledge and care; the draughtsman must know exactly what he means if his drawings are to be accurate and if they are to hang together. It has to be recollected that the ultimate intention of these geometrical drawings is their translation into stone, bricks, and mortar, or whatever material it may be, by a builder who, except for these drawings and the supplementary specification, is absolutely ignorant of what was in the designer's mind, and who at his best plays the rôle of an intelligent and conscientious translator. But what can the poor man do when he is brought up against vagaries such as wall-plates to an ordinary roof of narrow span measuring 12 inches by 10 inches, which I once saw in a drawing, or mouldings that would make even their author shudder if he had the slightest idea of the only possible result of his efforts when realised in practice? One cannot help wondering what must be the thoughts of experienced builders of the old-fashioned school when they come face to face with some of the drawings with which they have to deal. As to the numerous troubles which arise from the total discrepancy of plan, section, and elevation, or from the careless setting out of details of construction, these are so obvious that I need not dwell on them here, except to urge architectural students to bear constantly in mind that a loose, inaccurate working drawing is as culpable and mischievous as a loose, inaccurate statement of fact, and that it is no use a designer setting about a geometrical drawing till he is quite sure in his own mind what it is he wants to do, and how he is going to do it. In order to arrive at this, no amount of trouble should be spared in preliminary sketches.

The second condition—that the drawings should be perfectly clear—follows from the first. Certain vicious tendencies in architectural drawings have appeared in recent years, notably the use of a very thick line, and the use of a very thick line in connection with a much thinner line. The use of the thick line was in fashion when I was a student in the Academy thirty years ago, and was due to the medieval proclivities of William Burges, a fine draughtsman, spoilt by his fondness for posing. It was in 1860 that Burges read a paper on architectural drawing at the Royal Institute of British Architects, in which he advocated the use of " a good strong

thick bold line," as he put it, " so that we may get into the habit
of leaving out those prettinesses which only cost money and spoil
our design "—excellent advice, which he was the last man in the
world to follow himself. Street, who was present, suggested that
the whole thing was rubbish, and that every artist would find
his own line. Feeling ran high in those days, and Burges on
another occasion retorted that it was a pity Street could not
build his own cross-hatching. The real pity was that neither
of these considerable artists attempted to place himself in touch
with a reasonable tradition of drawing, and their labours have
been, in consequence, in vain. Burges deliberately copied the method
of a medieval draughtsman, with the result that what should have
been studies of fact were little more than exercises in style.

The second, and possibly even more injurious, use of the thick
line and the thin line has originated in competitions. In a room
full of drawings by different designers, competitors have feared
that their drawings would be overlooked unless some strong,
insistent line shouted its existence at the spectator. I have seen
lines on half-scale drawings measuring, by the scale, 2 inches in
thickness. Of course, with variations of lines such as this, not
only are all the refinements and subtleties of architecture lost,
but the breadth of effect goes too. Nor do I believe that such a
method makes any but an unfavourable impression on an assessor
who knows his business, and who, of course, reads the elevation
by the plan and section. As to the builder, the effect of such
methods of drawing must be simply paralysing. The line used
in geometrical drawings should be firmly drawn, uniform in thickness, sufficient to express neither more nor less than the architectural features intended. To put it another way, the designer
should have thought out exactly what he wants before he puts
his final line to paper, for the line so drawn becomes a business
datum of serious importance, as careless architects have found to

their cost when the damning evidence of an ill-considered line stares them in the face in their contract drawings.

I would warn students also against an abuse of skiography, which has become far too common in recent years; and that is, the habit of projecting violent shadows over every part of the plan. The result is that the drawings are illegible. I have seen plans which look like an arrangement of haycocks, in which the shadow of the column is far more prominent than the plan of the column itself. Nothing whatever is gained by this, and besides making the plan unreadable it also makes it very ugly. In geometrical drawings students should eschew all such tricks and devices, and be content to do a plain thing in a plain way.

The situation is almost reversed when we come to the second function of architectural drawing, that of producing in the mind of another the impression of an architectural idea. We are not concerned here with a bare and literal statement of facts. The impression aimed at is a complex one; that is, the draughtsman aims at producing the impression not only of certain abstract forms of architecture, but of those forms as a whole, and as a whole considered in relation to its placing on the site, its environment of sky and landscape, and even the intention of the building. All these matters have an important bearing on the value of the design, and their presentation is scarcely less essential than the data given by the working drawings, in the building up of the total impression to be conveyed to another mind. The line that in the geometrical drawing had to be hard and precise now becomes sensitive, even tentative, feeling its way and clinging on to the idea, as it were, in order to suggest it in all its multifarious complexity. Absolute and exhaustive accuracy of detail is less important here than accuracy in the statement as a whole. It may be found, in setting up a perspective of a building according to the strict rules of the art, that the result is disappointing;

somehow the building looks different from what had been expected, and if it has been carried out, from what it does look in fact. The explanation is that it is not only that the eye sees the buildings in perspective, but the brain takes its share in the process. Impressions are formed with lightning rapidity. Knowledge previously acquired comes into play; and unconsciously, because it is done so instantaneously, the mind jumps from what it sees to much that it does not see. The net result left in the mind by the observation of a building is its perspective modified by several other considerations. A draughtsman is justified, therefore, in taking these other considerations into account, emphasising part of the building in one place, modifying it in another; availing himself, in fact, of those principles of selection and restraint and suggestion which every artist has to employ in the statement of his impression. If, for example, he is dealing with an interior, and takes his station point inside the room or the hall—the only position from which the interior would, in fact, be visible—it will be found that unless it is a very long building, the perspective appears to be hopelessly exaggerated. It is usual, therefore, to place the station point outside the room, and one is justified in correcting the appearance of incorrectness. This must not, of course, be pushed to the extent of largely falsifying a building; the limits of the architectural draughtsman are more closely set than those of the free artist. But within those limits it is more important to convey the main idea than to give a literal and laborious transcript which, in fact, misrepresents the building.

In the third class of subjects—those in which the draughtsman uses architectural forms for the expression of abstract ideas—he is to all intents the free artist, with no limits to hamper him but those of his knowledge and imagination. In this class we are on the debatable ground that lies between architectural draughtsmanship and the province of the painter. Piranesi,

c

in his "prison" series, is the most remarkable instance of an artist who expressed ideas by means of architectural forms, where another artist might have attempted to do so by means of figures, and in a feebler form the tendency appears in Panini, Hubert Robert, and the eighteenth century painters of ruins.

Before I proceed to trace the development of architectural drawing and illustration, I should call the student's attention to a useful half-way house between the two extremes of geometrical drawings and perspective, and that is isometrical projection. The object of this is to show in one drawing, plan and elevation. The lines do not vanish in either case, so that the drawing is not in perspective, though at first sight it has some appearance of it, and it is this that differentiates it from drawings where the plan, though shown with the elevation, is set out in perspective, such as the beautiful drawing by Bramante in the Uffizi Gallery at Florence of a project for St. Peter's. The usual method of isometrical projection is to set down to scale the ground and upper plans square to the bottom line of the picture, and one above and behind the other, on a guide line set out to an angle of 45 degrees, or whatever angle best shows the purpose of the building. On this guide line the heights of the features which it is intended to show are set out to the scale of the plan and the lines ruled off from these points. In Spiers and Anderson's *Architecture of Greece and Rome* there is a masterly isometrical view of the Colosseum by Guadet, which shows what an immense amount of information can be given in one drawing by the use of this process. In the illustration facing p. 12 from Choisy's *Art de Bâtir chez les Romains* there is a variation in the method described above, the plan being set out at an angle. Choisy used this method freely to illustrate his *History of Architecture*.

Purpose of Architectural Drawing 11

Though architecture is in one sense the oldest of the arts, architectural drawing, as we know it, is comparatively modern. I do not doubt that when Ictinus designed the Parthenon, a setting out of the most delicate accuracy must have been made; those subtleties of outline and profile, the rules of which have only been discovered and determined by the careful calculations of expert students, could never have been carried out by rule of thumb or by eye. Nor, again, is it possible to conceive of the great Roman Thermæ being set out without very careful plans; but any such plans have necessarily perished, and it is a regrettable fact that from time immemorial little attention has been paid to architects' drawings, masterpieces of technical dexterity and draughtsmanship though they have often been. When the building was once up nobody cared about the drawings; but one would sacrifice a good many bad pictures for the working drawings of the Baths of Caracalla. Vitruvius refers to the drawing of plan and elevation in a very cursory manner, but no record or any fragment, even of a plan, has reached us, unless we include the marble plan of Rome, which Vespasian and afterwards Severus set up in the Templum Sacræ Urbis.

With the gradual break-up of the Roman Empire most of the secrets of an older art were lost. Architecture split up into East and West, and the best of it went East; but we know little or nothing of the methods of practice of the Byzantine architects. Anthemius of Tralles is described as the architect of Santa Sophia, but his actual title was "μηχανο-ποιός," the maker of machines and devices, less of the architect than the engineer and builder. The Romanesque buildings show little trace of the architect's pencil. Vigorous and picturesque as many of them were, they were yet such as could have been built by masons on the general instruction of a superior authority. The mere diagram plan with inscriptions of the monastery of St. Gall, made in the ninth century, is an instance,* and such, in fact, continued to be the practice of building till well into the Middle Ages. There is, I believe, no evidence for supposing that William of Wykeham was an architect or, indeed, other than an influential and highly intelligent person who organised the finance and conduct of important building enterprises, and was, in fact, in the position of the patron, or client, as we call him, not in that of either the modern architect or builder. Here, indeed, we are met by a difficult problem. The intricacies of Gothic vaulting, the setting out of groining-ribs, liernes, tercerets, and the like, tax the best abilities of the modern draughtsman, and it is difficult to imagine that no general scheme, plan, section, and elevation of cathedrals so complete and homogeneous as Salisbury or Lincoln was prepared and on the works throughout the periods of their building ; yet authentic examples of real working drawings, with proper plans and sections, as well as elevations, are extremely rare, if they exist at all. There are certain drawings of the cathedrals of Siena and Cologne, and there are the two elevations of the west front of the Cathedral of Orvieto, supposed to have been made by Lorenzo del Maitano of Siena soon after 1310, when he was appointed *capo-mæstro* of the Duomo. These drawings, which were not carried out, are not really working drawings, inasmuch as they are set out in slight perspective which, though not correct, is near enough to make one doubt whether they can be as early as 1310, and one's suspicions are heightened by the precision of the draughtsmanship and the fine drawings of the figures in the tympanum of the central archway. The designs are in the Italian manner of Gothic, with rectangular compartments for carving, which assort ill with the pinnacles, gables, and floriated crockets of the upper part of the design.

* Burges describes this in the paper I have referred to ; but by no stretch of imagination could it be considered a working drawing.

Isometrical Drawing. By A. Choisy. From *L'Art de Bâtir chez les Romains*

"The Maze," &c. (p. XVII) By Villard de Honnecourt

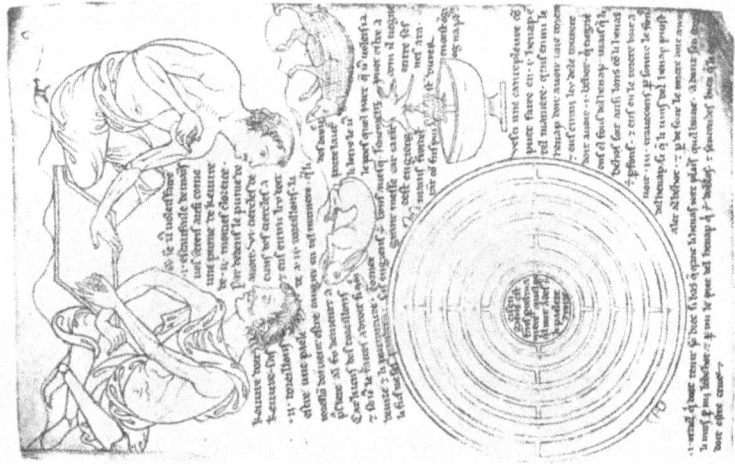

Detail of Stall End (p. LVII) By Villard de Honnecourt

These drawings are, I believe, the nearest approach to a working drawing to be found in the Middle Ages; but I doubt if they were made with that object, or that the necessity for working drawings was seriously felt by the Gothic builders. On the other hand, that there were men who could draw, and draw very well, is proved by the famous sketch-book of Villard de Honnecourt. This book was once in the possession of Felibien, the well-known historiographer of Louis XIV., and though he appears to have known little about its origin, he was too good a judge not to realise the remarkable quality of its draughtsmanship, and that at a time when Le Brun was dictator of the arts in France and J. H. Mansart its leading architect. Attention was drawn to the book by Quicherat in 1849, and when Lassus and Darcel reproduced the little album by lithography in 1858, and Willis's annotated edition appeared in 1859, most of the Gothic revivalists regarded it as the revelation of a new heaven and a new earth; the sanction, in fact, to the ingenious hypotheses which they had hitherto evolved from their inner consciousness. But its effect was, I think, to make their art even more unreal and histrionic than it was before, because they mistook the lesson to be learnt from the studies of this artist, who drew what he liked in his own natural manner and as he saw it. For the methods of presentation which may be sincere and genuine in one age become mere conventions in another; tricks of drawing that have lost their meaning, because they have been divorced from the patient observation of facts. Yet Burges was so delighted that he set to work to make a vellum sketch-book of his own in the manner of de Honnecourt—a volume of thirty-six sheets, bound in green leather as a pocket-book, and now in the library of the Royal Institute of British Architects. This he filled with drawings of elephants, rhinoceros, birds and beasts, the Rose of Sharon, heartsease and honeysuckle, crockets, gargoyles, scraps of architecture, fancy heads, all drawn in that "good strong thick bold line," as Burges called it, one cannot help feeling, with an eye to their effect on the page and the verisimilitude of the Gothic manner, rather than as searching studies of forms. It was a pity, because Burges could draw very well when he took the trouble. It was a pity, too, that nobody, in fact, knew anything about Villard de Honnecourt, and not even to a century when he was born. That he was an observant and most spirited draughtsman is shown by his sketches, drawn in ink on vellum with a strong, trenchant line; and nothing came amiss to Villard—men and animals, stags, lions, sheep and horses, ostriches, eagles, grasshoppers, flying buttresses, bays of Rheims Cathedral, mouldings and details of architecture, a drawing of the Tower of Laon with the famous cows, the apse of Cambrai, and one or two sheets of figures set out in geometrical diagrams, exercises in design which had a peculiar fascination for artists down to the middle of the sixteenth century. Probably Villard was not an architect as we should understand the term, but he was an artist, and the arts were not differentiated in the thirteenth and fourteenth centuries. He drew whatever took his fancy, and in nearly all his drawings there is the same keen vitality. The two figures wrestling suggest a professional wrestling match more vividly than any photograph, because the artist has seen and realised the essential qualities of such a contest, and has given us a summary statement, symbolical of wrestling matches in general, of the watching for an opening, the tense strain of adversaries playing for the final grip. The same quality of line and selection appears in the admirable drawing of a swan, and the strange-looking creature above it, rather like a sloth with its great claws. Another figure here reproduced (facing p. 15) tells its story with pathetic intensity—a brief note of the utter abandonment of despair.

These drawings deserve the careful study of the architectural student, not as models for imitation, but as examples of what may

"The Wrestlers" (p. XXVIII.) By Villard de Honnecourt

"The Swan" (p. VII.) By Villard de Honnecourt

A Chevet and Figure (p. XXXIII.)   By Villard
de Honnecourt

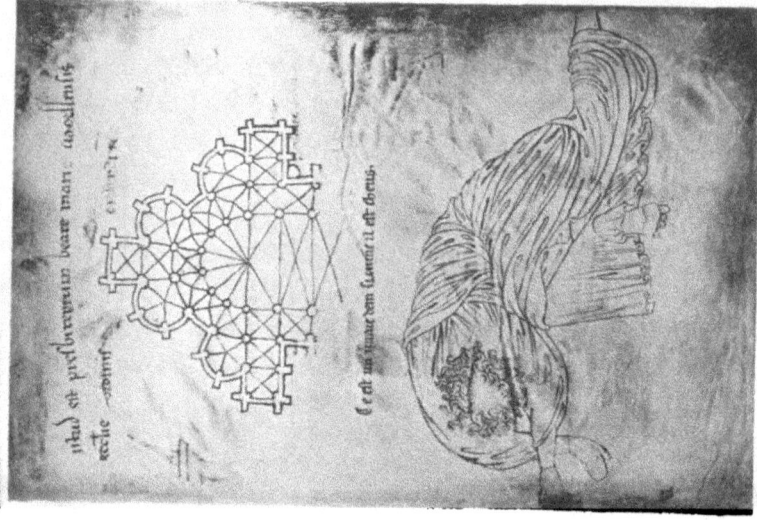

Figure of a King (p. XLIX.)   By Villard
de Honnecourt

be done in drawing by very simple means, if these means are based on personal study and observation, and inspired by real conviction.   It must not be supposed for an instant that these drawings are the work of an immature man, but Villard could not escape the tradition of his time.   He belonged to the school of those artists who designed the glorious windows of Bourges and Chartres, men who concealed under a rather formal convention strong feeling and a burning imagination, and Villard de Honnecourt must have observed much and drawn a great deal before he could have reached this power and flexibility of line.   To a modern architectural student the plans of apses and chevets, indicated in rough freehand, may seem loose and ragged, and so they are ; but they were probably not intended for more than the briefest notes, to remind Villard of places that he had seen and admired. And if it came to carrying them out, it is quite possible that little more than such rough indications as these would have been given to the builder, complete and well-founded reliance being placed on the traditional knowledge of the master masons.   For as between people with full knowledge a mere hint may be enough. These rough sketch plans are the work of a man who knew what he was about, and only an artist who had studied these matters closely would have been able to set down one of these complicated plans in correct proportion.   To the architectural draughtsman, more particularly, drawing is the expression of knowledge and the symbol of a fund of accumulated observations, and one finds both in these medieval drawings and in the drawings of the earlier men of the Renaissance, the same power of selecting and indicating the essential parts of an architectural design.   There is no labour wasted in mechanical finish.   The draughtsman had in his own mind a clear idea of what he intended to convey, and eliminated all that was superfluous or could in any way obscure the lucidity of its expression.   There is in the work of these earlier men a certain abstract austerity of statement which will disappear under the more complicated conditions of later architecture.

No doubt there were other artists and designers in the Middle Ages as capable as Villard de Honnecourt : Eudes de Montreuil, and Hugh Libergiers, for example, and others, who are no more than names, may have been such men ; but they and their drawings are unknown to us. So far as the individual artist is concerned, there seems to be no lifting of the veil of the Middle Ages. We do not know the names even of the sculptors of Rheims and Auxerre, of Amiens or Notre Dame, or of the artist of the windows of Bourges, or of the jewellers, enamellers, illuminators—those incomparable artists whose masterpieces afford us glimpses, far too rare, of a world of astonishing beauty and not less astonishing remoteness from ourselves. Had it been necessary to prepare elaborate working drawings, there can be little doubt that in a period so rich in art there were men who were capable of doing it. The probable explanation is that such drawings were not necessary, and that the tradition of building that undoubtedly existed among workmen and the tradition of design preserved by the clergy, rendered elaborate architectural drawings unnecessary. When there was only one manner of building conceivable, both to builder and owner, general instructions from the latter were enough, the rest was done by the mason working his stones and setting them out on the building as it grew.

At the end of the fifteenth century, when Gothic art was drawing to its close, there were men who could set up a geometrical elevation of a Gothic façade. In Egger's collection there are a few German drawings to scale, and one (facing p. 17), which I reproduce, is a drawing of considerable excellence, such as could only have been made by somebody who had been accustomed to geometrical drawing, and who perfectly understood the setting out of tracery. This is, however, I believe, a rare example of a working drawing

A page from Burges's Vellum Sketch Book. In the Collection of the Royal Institute of British Architects

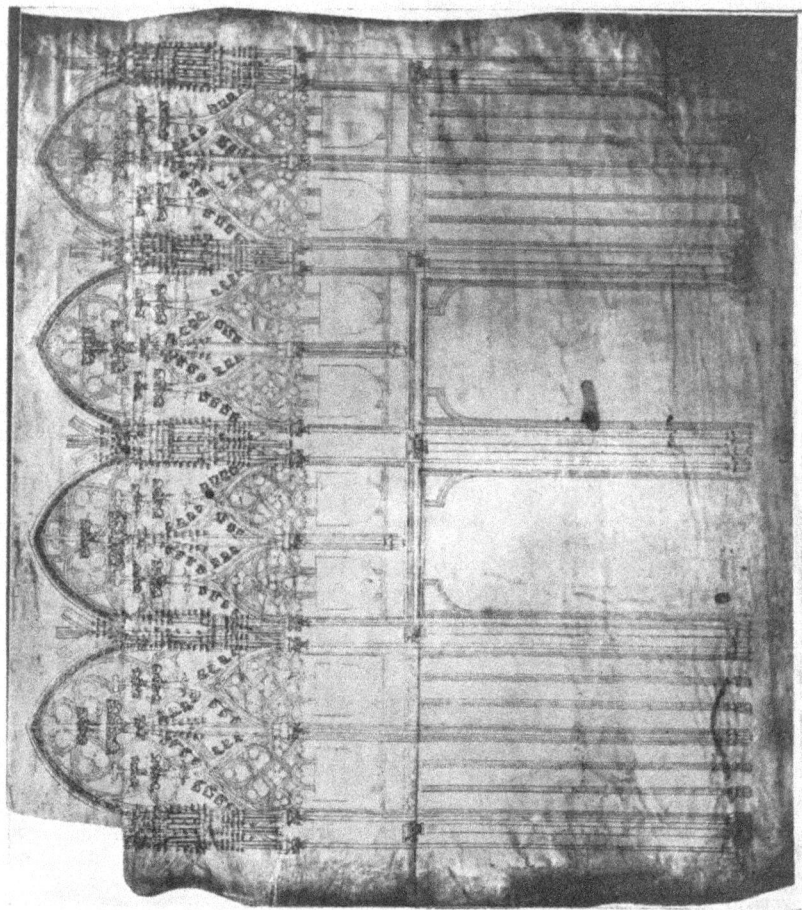

A German Drawing (end of Fifteenth Century) from Egger. *Architektonische Handzeichnungen*

of the fifteenth century. I know of no similar instances in French or English Gothic, and incline to think that details were set out full size and straight away on the building. It is probable that the only instructions given were general directions to the work-men to follow some familiar example. Even in the fifteenth century it is not to be supposed that a man like Sir Reginald Bray worked at a drawing-board, like a modern architect, when he had to deal with the Chapel of Henry VII. His share was to organise and administer, and to decide on the general purpose and character of his building. The workman, with an immemorial tradition behind him, would have no difficulty in interpreting directions so given, and though he might modify his detail here and there, and perhaps introduce some fancy of his own, he would not conceive of the possibility of serious deviation from a well-marked path. As we shall see, in modern architecture this has been reversed. In the early days of the Renaissance, architecture was to a great extent an exotic, introduced and run, if we may so put it, by scholars. It had to be explained, down to its minutest detail, to unlearned and ignorant men, and thus architectural draughts-manship, which had little or no place in medieval times, became and remains an absolute necessity in neo-classic architecture.

It might be an interesting speculation to consider how far some of the qualities of medieval architecture were due to the absence of organised working drawings : its informality, its habit of improvisation in detail, its irregularities and neglect of sym-metry in design. The implicit reliance on drawings in modern practice would certainly account for much of the mechanical quality of modern Gothic. For Gothic architecture was essentially a builder's art ; that is to say, its whole scheme and conduct were local, initiated and practised on the spot, not administered from a distance ; and this had one immense advantage, that the designers worked in the concrete, not in the abstract—they saw

D

what they were doing, and could test and alter their programme as the work went along. Our modern Gothic architects have been trained, not in the workshop and on scaffolding, but in architects' offices and schools. They have no means of conveying their ideas to the builder but through a system of drawing which came into existence for the purpose of a quite different method of design. It is no doubt impossible nowadays to carry out a Gothic design except by means of the usual working drawings; but I cannot help thinking that here, as in other regards, the modern Gothic designer is kicking against the pricks, and would be wiser to submit to the inevitable and design his buildings in a manner less dependent on details and more on abstract qualities of line and proportion which it is possible to convey to the builder by means of careful working drawings.

CHAPTER II

ARCHITECTURAL DRAUGHTSMEN OF THE SIXTEENTH CENTURY :
BRAMANTE—THE SAN GALLO—THE DU CERCEAU—DE L'ORME

ARCHITECTURAL drawing, as we now understand it, really dates
from the earlier days of the Italian Renaissance. I do not know
if there are any drawings of Alberti in existence, but there are
drawings by Bramante, and a considerable number by Giuliano
da San Gallo, his brother Antonio, his son Antonio—the latter an
admirable draughtsman—Peruzzi, and others. This takes us back,
in the case of the two first, to the latter part of the fifteenth
century. I shall return to these men later. There are also, of
course, the painters—Mantegna (1430–1506), Carlo Crivelli (1468–
93), Pinturicchio (1454–1513), Ghirlandajo (1449–98), Signorelli
(1441–1524), Liberale da Verona (1451–1535), Borgognone of
Milan, Carpaccio, and others. There are fine examples in the
National Gallery : the " Annunciation," by Crivelli, with its
courts and the arcaded gallery with the carpet hung over
the parapet, and the peacock on the cornice ; or " The Death
of Dido," by Liberale da Verona, in which the drawing of the
architecture is as crisp as that of Guardi himself ; or the triumphal
arch and that delightful loggia in " The Story of Griselda," by
an unknown Umbrian painter.

These men used architecture freely in their compositions and
with obvious enjoyment in its design, and gave it with a full-
ness of presentation very different from the abstract summaries
of medieval frescoes. The architecture in the background of
their pictures is beautifully conceived, and sometimes only second

in interest to the actual subject of the picture, for these artists of the Renaissance were enthusiasts for the new architecture that scholars were discovering for them from the remains of ancient Rome, and their ingenuous minds were fascinated by experiments with the newly formulated rules of perspective. All these painters were humanists in their way—men who thought about their art and were keenly alive to its many-sided problems ; painters who realised in a way that has been forgotten in modern times that the Arts, though separate, are also related, and that the artist should be alive to beauty in every art and in other arts than his own. Architecture has been used, and admirably used, as a background for their pictures by many painters since those days ; but the point of view has altered, and it is a far cry back from the columns and curtains of Mignard and Le Brun to the fantastic courts and galleries of Carlo Crivelli.

Architecture, as handled by the Italian painters of the earlier Renaissance, would be an interesting study, well worth the attention of painter students ; but it is outside my present subject, and I merely note that these men, by their enthusiasm and architecture, contributed to the spreading of new ideas, and also in a special degree to the education of the humbler artist who was striving to illustrate Vitruvius and Alberti. The profiles and sections in Crivelli's " Annunciation " suggest the types given in the early printed books of architecture, their immaturity and over-accentuation.

We left Villard de Honnecourt at some unknown date in the Middle Ages, an accomplished artist in his way, yet hardly, except in a summary and rudimentary manner, an architectural draughtsman. I take him, from internal evidence, to have been wandering about France with his sketch-book early in the fourteenth century. After him, we draw the Middle Ages blank, with the exceptions I have noted and unimportant German exceptions at the end of the fifteenth century. Indeed, one might say with reasonable probability that architectural draughtsmanship did not exist, the necessity for it not having as yet arisen in the practice of architecture. But meanwhile in Italy there had come about that astonishing outburst of intellectual activity which we call quite vaguely " the Renaissance." Scholars had revealed the splendour and the beauty of the ancient world, and the Arts were no longer the expression of centuries of tradition moving by imperceptible degrees, but represented the play of each man's mind on the subject of his choice, and became to a great extent a matter of personal revelation and initiative. The mere indications adequate in medieval architecture were useless when designers wished to build in a manner unknown to the ordinary workman. More than that, the designer had to master that manner himself, by unremitting study of the innumerable fragments of ancient architecture still left in Italy. The famous album of Giuliano da San Gallo is almost entirely devoted to studies of the antique, and throughout the sixteenth century Serlio, Palladio, Vignola, De l'Orme, Du Perac, Bullant, and a host of other enthusiastic students, spent years in collecting details of the antique, some by genuine research on the spot, others by cribbing freely from each other's sketch-books. It was owing to this emancipation of the individual and to this radical change in the aims and methods of architecture that architectural draughtsmanship came into existence. It is, by its very nature, essentially a modern art, the complement of methods of architecture and archæology which were undreamt of in the Middle Ages, for it was the revival of scholarship that brought about the study of archæology, and the two together that revolutionised architecture.

The astonishing thing is that architectural draughtsmanship should appear in Italy, completely equipped, within certain limits, in the latter part of the fifteenth century. The earliest example that I know is a drawing in the Uffizi Gallery by Brunelleschi, who died in 1446. Except that the Corinthian pilaster is fifteen diameters high, it is a perfectly competent drawing ; but the Renaissance was beginning to move fast, and we now come to Giuliano da San Gallo, Fra Giocondo, and Bramante, men who were almost exact contemporaries, Fra Giocondo and Bramante dying in 1515, and the elder San Gallo the year after. In the Vatican Library there is an album of drawings by Giuliano da San Gallo, the ablest of the elder generation of that famous family.* The drawings, seventy-six in number, are made in pen and ink on sheepskin sheets 1 foot 6 inches by 1 foot 3⅜ inches wide, evidently a *liber aureus*, in which only the most highly prized examples of architecture were to be included. There are one or two designs by San Gallo himself, but most of his subjects are taken from the ruins of Roman buildings in Italy. The date on the cartouche on the title page is 1465, but it appears that the book was only put together in 1490, as it includes a plan and elevation of a palace designed by San Gallo for Lorenzo di Medici in 1488, and it was not till 1490 that Lorenzo officially allowed him the title of " da San Gallo." There are, moreover, differences in the draughtsmanship. Some of the earlier drawings are crude, and San Gallo never drew the figure well, but in many of the drawings the profiles are firm and unfaltering, and the details are drawn with clearness and precision, as, for instance, the sheet of capitals which I reproduce. Here one gets, for the first time, the method of drawing architectural details which became general in printed books of architecture of the following century ; and in its directness of statement and scholarly selection of essential features this is, in some respects, a model for technical book illus-

---

* See G. Clausse, "*Giamberti*" (*Antonio*) *called Da San Gallo* for a detailed description of this album and of the drawings by the elder San Gallo at Florence and Vienna. The album has been reproduced in facsimile by Otto Hannassowitz (Leipzig, 1900).

Sheet of details of the Colosseum. By Giuliano da San Gallo. From the
Libro da Giuliano da San Gallo, Vatican Library

Drawing by Giuliano da San Gallo. From the *Libro da Giuliano da San Gallo,*
Vatican Library

tration. The forms are given with a firm yet flexible line, with a minimum of shading and without any trace of that passion for elaborate finish which was introduced by the French draughtsmen of Louis XIV., and which never seems to have appealed to the Italian temperament. These men were out after facts and their simplest record, and they passed on from one freshly discovered or invented detail to another, impatient in their search for knowledge, careless almost of the effect of their drawings, and yet they did extremely well what they set out to do. In San Gallo's drawings there is no fumbling about for the forms of architecture, no misapprehension of their logical purpose, such as are almost inevitable when the draughtsman does not understand what he is drawing. San Gallo was a well-trained architect who knew very well what he was about—namely, the accumulation of materials for the technique of the neo-classic. He appears, in this respect resembling Villard de Honnecourt, to have wandered about and drawn whatever took his fancy. There is a fine plan of Santa Sophia, and a characteristic section on which he has drawn a mermaid holding a ship, perhaps a note of his wanderings beyond the seas. On the other hand, Giuliano da San Gallo had his limitations; though he was a conscientious and accurate draughtsman of astonishing skill if we consider the state of architecture elsewhere, he was destitute, it seems, of that imaginative insight which makes some architects' sketches so delightfully suggestive and personal. The ten drawings by him in the Uffizi Gallery, in outline and tint, show the same methodical care; his work has little of the quality possessed in a high degree by his great contemporary Bramante and by the two most distinguished architects of the next generation, Baldassare Peruzzi and his own son Antonio da San Gallo the younger. Still, in its scholarship and zeal for knowledge, the book of Giuliano da San Gallo marks the opening of a new outlook on architecture, from which tremendous developments were to follow in the future, that untiring research into the architecture of the past which has been ever since an essential element of every architect's training.

The collection of plans and details, generally known as "The Sketch-book of Andreas Coner," now in the Soane Museum, is another example, richer in plans than the work of San Gallo. Nothing is known of Coner, and the collection is called by his name only on account of a letter from him to Bernardo Rucellai, dated Rome, September 1st, 1513, a copy of which appears in the book. There were certainly two artists at work in this collection, and probably three or four.*

In the Uffizi Gallery there is a drawing in outline and tint by Fra Giocondo.† It is well drawn, but chiefly remarkable for the very fine sketch in ink of a figure leaning back much foreshortened. Bramante has nine characteristic drawings at the Uffizi, notably that perspective study in plan and elevation of a project for St. Peter's, to which I referred in my first chapter ‡ an admirable and most workmanlike drawing, which not only shows very closely the designer's intention, but suggests that a certain roughness and carelessness, which I have noted in others of his drawings, was temperamental, and not in the least degree due to inexactness of thought or want of dexterity. The work, however, that shows most clearly Bramante's power as an architectural draughtsman is the magnificent engraving in the British Museum, of which only one other copy is known to exist. The plate measures 2 feet 4 inches high by 1 foot 8 inches wide, and is not dated. It represents the interior of a temple or hall, with two vaulted aisles, of which the upper part is shown broken and

---

* See the Introduction by Dr. Ashby and the reproductions in facsimile issued by the British School at Rome in 1904.

† See *Disegni di Architettura Civile et Militare* in the Uffizi Gallery, Florence, published by Giacomo Brogi (Florence, 1907).

‡ Brogi, Plate VIII.

Capitals and Details. By Giuliano da San Gallo. From the *Libro da*
Giuliano San Gallo, Vatican Library

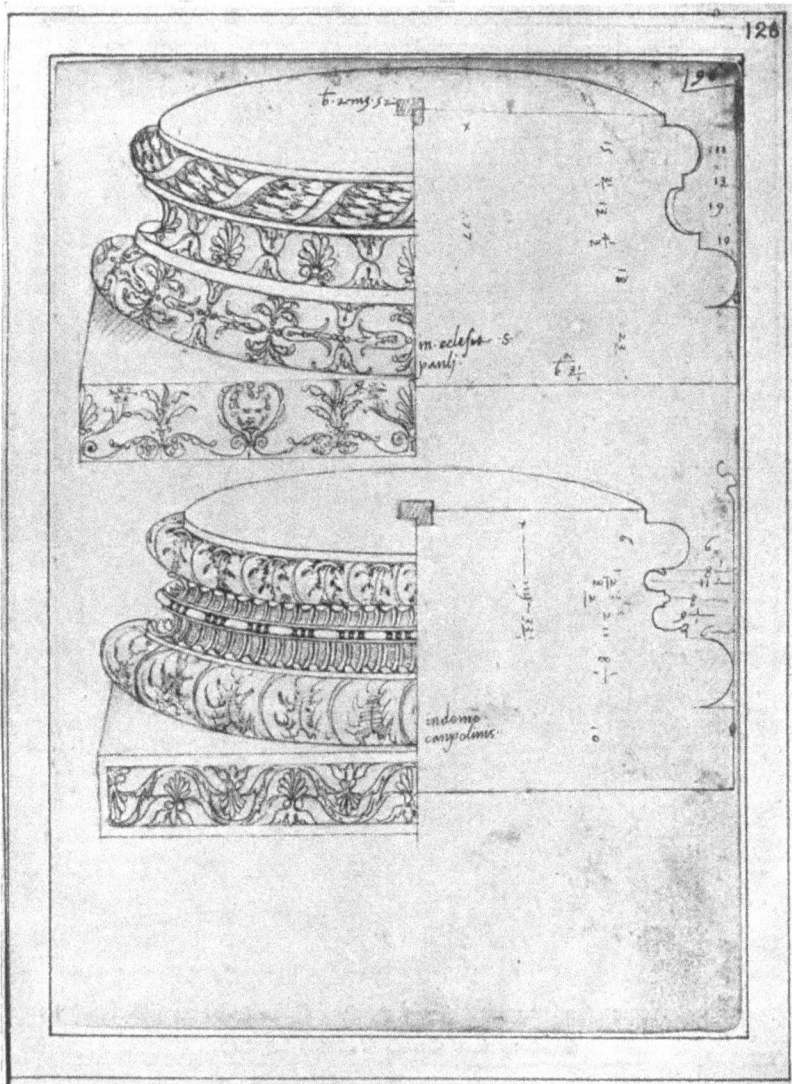

From " The Book of Andreas Coner." Soane Museum

Engraving by Bramante. In the British Museum

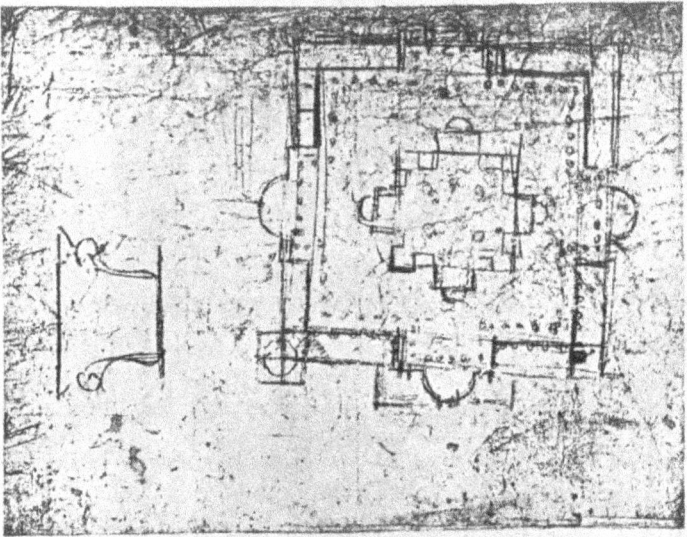

Sheet of Studies by Bramante and Peruzzi. From De Geymüller's *Primitive Projects for St. Peter's at Rome,* Plate XVIII

ruinous. In the foreground is the kneeling figure of an old man, with head and forepart of a horse on the right, and young men in the dress of the time standing about beyond. In the centre of the left aisle is a candelabrum on a pedestal on two steps, and the aisle ends in a half octagon apse, with a great shell upside down in the semi-dome. In the tympanum of the arch above is a circular opening through which is shown the back of a bust. It is a strange drawing, of which the meaning is obscure; but it shows a rare faculty of chastened architectural design, and a technique based on that of his master, Andrea Mantegna, and scarcely inferior to the work of that incomparable artist. I do not desire to draw invidious comparisons when I call attention to the difference of intellectual and imaginative outlook shown in this engraving as compared with the drawings made by Villard de Honnecourt, say two hundred years before, the medievalist noting his details with child-like candour, and also with a vivacity of observation given only to children, and the man of the Renaissance in the plenitude of his skill and knowledge, searching for hidden meanings, living again in a half imaginary world of the past.

Giuliano da San Gallo, his brother, his son Antonio, and Bramante and his pupils may be taken as the founders of archi-tectural drawing, and their drawings, as compared with the work of later draughtsmen, have an almost archaic purity of line. In the collection of projects for St. Peter's at Rome, published by de Geymüller in 1875, there are reproductions of drawings by all these men, and the differences of method are characteristic. Bramante's own drawings are impatient and masterful—rough notes of what was passing in his mind rather than finished studies. His plan of St. Peter's is sketched in chalk on squared paper, and in the freehand drawing of St. Pietro in Montorio he has not taken the trouble to set out the circular perspective of the stairs with any approach to accuracy. Bramante's powers, both as a designer

E

and a draughtsman, are beyond question ; but Peruzzi, his pupil and assistant, and the greatest of the Renaissance architects, went more to the root of the matter in the drawings which he made for Bramante, as in that splendid and characteristic sheet of plan and perspective sketches made in 1505-6. At the Uffizi there are seven drawings by Peruzzi, including the plan of the Massimi Palace to scale, a finely drawn sheet of details, and a remarkable perspective showing certain of the ancient buildings combined in one drawing, an exercise of which the architects of the Renaissance were very fond, and which continued in use down to the eighteenth century. Among the drawings attributed to Raphael in the same collection is an admirable drawing of a Doric vestibule, with a seated figure of a soldier on the step in the foreground, which is probably by Peruzzi. This artist and Antonio da San Gallo the younger possessed an extraordinary freedom of drawing in pen-and-ink. In de Geymüller's collection of projects for St. Peter's there are some delightful little perspective studies of architectural motives by the younger San Gallo. These side notes and sketches seem to me exactly the sort of thing that students ought to aim at in working out their designs, trial flights of imagination, realisations of the effect in perspective of the geometrical design. If the designer has not clearly in his mind what he is about, he ought to visualise his ideas by rough sketches of the blocking and composition of his building, and this will often reveal unexpected difficulties and, on the other hand, valuable motives of design. The skill and trueness of hand shown in these suggestive sketches are a striking testimony to the great ability of the younger San Gallo, and to the range of his knowledge of architectural forms.

That such drawings could only be made by a man who was both a fine draughtsman and a master of architecture is proved by two examples. In the library of the Royal Institute of British Architects there is a volume of sketch designs for

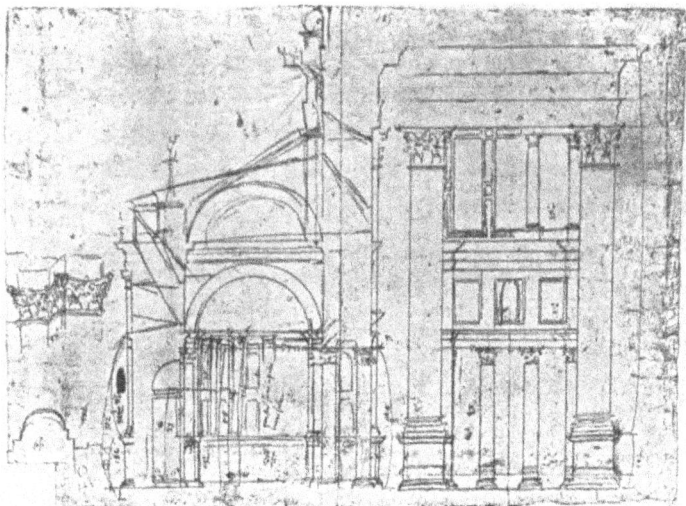

Studies by Antonio da San Gallo. From de Geymüller's *Primitive Projects for St. Peter's at Rome* (1875), Pl. 35

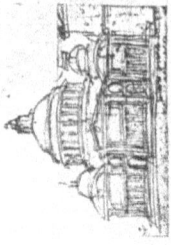

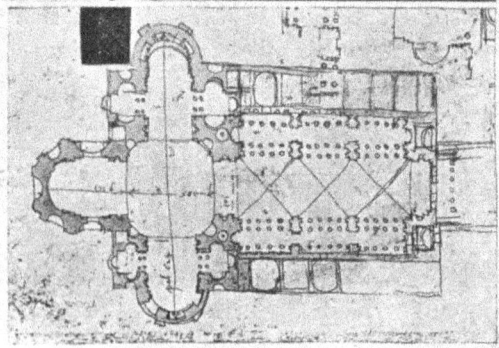

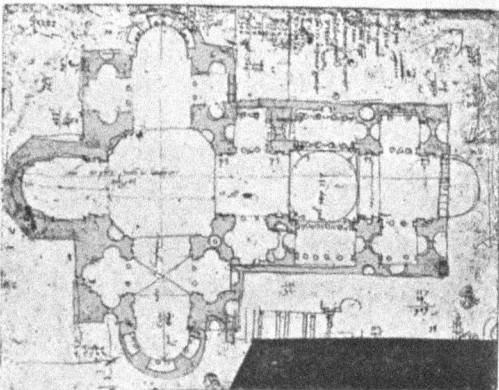

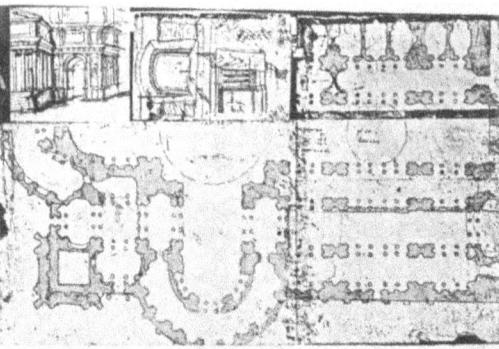

Studies by Peruzzi for Bramante. From De Geymüller's *Primitive Projects for St. Peter's at Rome,*
Plate 20

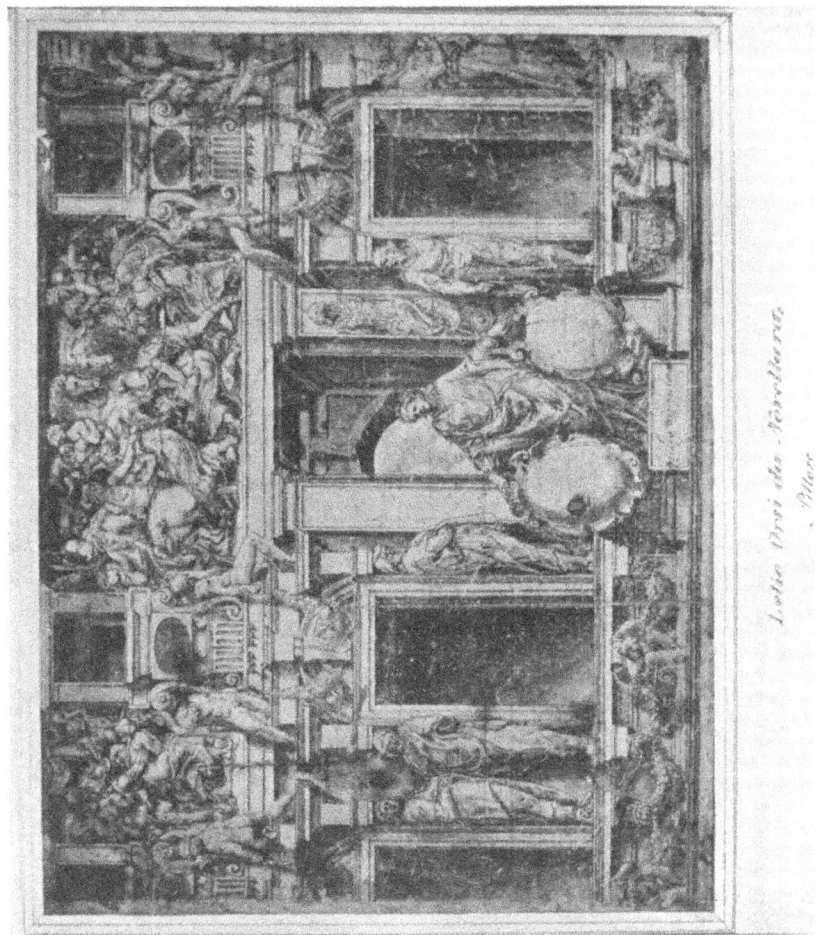

Design for Wall Decoration. Drawing attributed to Lelio Orsi da Novellara. In the Laing Bequest, National Gallery of Scotland

...g..., comme ie vous ay dict çy deſſus. Vous n'y ſçauriez faillir, pourueu que vous teniez vos pieces les plus courtes que pourrez: lignamment au bois lequel cognoiſtrez eſtre plus fragil & fian‑ gible. Le tout pouuez voir & iuger par la figure qui s'enſuit.

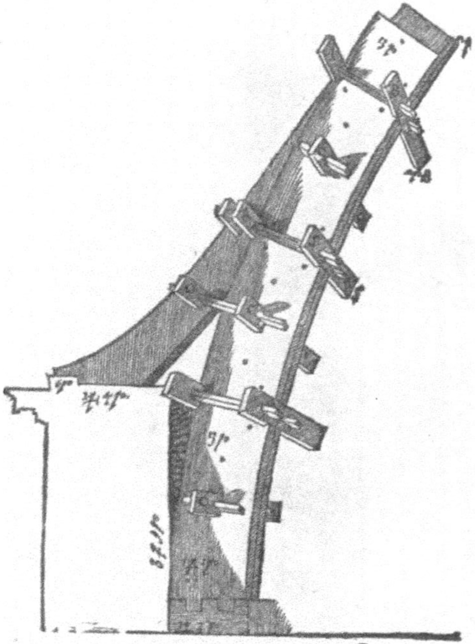

Ggg ij

Detail of Roof. By Philibert De l'Orme. *Nouvelles Inventions, etc.*, X. 292. (Regnault Chaudiere's Edition)

NONVS. 83

rint, vti percolatiõibus aquæ tranſmutari poſſint, multo ſalubriori & vſu efficient, Limus enim cũ habuerit quo ſubſidat, limpidior aqua fiet, & ſine odoribus conſeruabit ſaporem, ſi non ſalé addi neceſſe erit, & extenuari.

c. moztacï

a. Fiſtuca ſeu uectes lignei b. opus figulinũ

Quæ potui de aq virtute & varietate, qſq habeat vtilitates, quibuſq ratio nibus ducatur & pbetur, In hoc uolumine poſui, de gnomonicis vero re/ bus & horologiorum rationibus inſequenti perſcribam.

Opus Signinum. P. 83. Jocundus's Edition of *Vitruvius* (Venice, 1511)

buildings by Chambers and Yenn. Chambers was the famous architect of Somerset House, and Yenn, though an uninteresting person, arrived at the dignity of a Royal Academician. Yet their drawings are ragged and ignorant compared with such sketches as those of San Gallo. Their authors, whether Chambers or Yenn, or both, lacked the grip of architecture, the sureness of line, which distinguishes the work of the Italian. The other example is a painter. In de Geymüller's collection there is a reproduction of a sheet of drawings of domed churches attributed to Leonardo da Vinci. I do not know if the attribution is correct, but the drawing is as uncertain as the half-thought-out ideas they attempt to indicate, and if the drawing is authentic it would dispose once and for all of the claims of that great artist to architectural attainment—claims, indeed, which have never been substantiated by any evidence worth the name. I refer to this because not only students, but many others often fail to realise the fact that the power of drawing architecture well is, to this extent, on all fours with the power of drawing the figure well, and is only to be obtained in both cases by close observation and hard-won knowledge. As a fine example of figure drawing and architecture, in which both are understood and handled by a master, I give the remarkable drawing in the collection of the Scottish National Gallery, attributed to Lelio Orsi da Novellara (1511–87).

Architectural draughtsmanship, as handled by the men I have named, was now mature and as complete as was necessary for their purpose ; but at about this time—at the beginning, that is, of the sixteenth century—a fresh factor, of vast possibilities, appears in the printed and illustrated books of architecture. The first illustrated edition of Vitruvius was published at Venice by Johannes de Tridino, alias Tacuino, in 1511, with the title of *M. Vitruvius per Jocundum Solito Castigatior factus, cum figuris et Tabula ut jam legi et intelligi possit.* This modest expectation was imperfectly fulfilled, as may be seen from the illustration (p. 83) of " Opus signinum," the laying of concrete foundations. In the rare little Giunta edition of 1513 the illustrations are rougher still. The draughtsmanship here exhibited was at first and for many years a very humble affair. It seems surprising, after Bramante's magnificent engraving, that the early editions of Vitruvius should have been illustrated as crudely as they were. The limitations of the wood-block engraver had a good deal to do with it ; but I also suspect that those enterprising houses, Johannes de Tridino of Venice, Philippus di Giunta of Florence, and Fezandat of Paris, did not care to pay the price demanded by really competent men. As a matter of fact, these architectural illustrations were extremely rough. The draughtsman had not yet made up his mind whether he was drawing geometrical elevations or a perspective, so he combined the two. On the other hand, in illustrating the life of prehistoric man as described by Vitruvius, he was capable of such fancy drawings as that on p. 13 (edition of 1511), and he evidently felt much more at his ease with the ram's head of the battering-rams, than with the Corinthian and Ionic orders. The details of classical architecture were still very strange to the illustrator. In the *Hypnerotomachia* (1499) the architecture is altogether inferior to the figure, nor did it improve to any appreciable extent in the next generation.

The first genuine advance in architectural illustration seems to have been made by Serlio in his *Architettura*. Serlio was not a fine draughtsman in any sense, but he followed Giuliano da San Gallo in the critical spirit and the anxiety to get at the facts with which he applied himself to the study and presentation of architecture. The fine plan and section and the sheet of elevation and details of the Colosseum are pretty much what an intelligent student of architecture might endeavour to make at the present

Sheet of Details from the Colosseum.   By Sebastiano Serlio (Venice, 1544)

Quest'ordine Composito, cio e capitello architrave fregio
et cornice è piu cauato da diuersi luoghi fra le antiquita di
Roma et ridotto aproportione come fidetto del Corinto: il
quale per essere diligentemente notato per memori da se si
mostra

X X V IIII.

Plate XXVII. *Regola delle Cinque Ordini.* By Giacomo Barrozzio da Vignola

day, allowing for the exigencies of the woodcut. Here, again, if one compares them with the architectural detail of Villard de Honnecourt, the difference between the medievalist and the men of the Renaissance is apparent, the first just noting the idea of an apse in single line, the second measuring, conscientiously plotting the plan even of so huge a building as the Colosseum, and supplementing this with careful studies of the detail. Serlio's *Libro Terzo* was a memorable achievement, and set the type of architectural illustration in Italy for the rest of the century. The curious thing is that he himself lost touch of it in the dull and laboured plates of his *Extraordinario Libro*, published at Lyons in 1551 ; but Serlio had failed at the French Court, and perhaps this book represented the desperate effort of a broken man., Palladio followed the methods of the *Libro Terzo* with a great deal of skill and not infrequent lapses into the banalities of his individual manner ; but his details are clearly drawn, and he had an excellent sketchy way of indicating the plans and elevations of his houses. Palladio was, in fact, an accomplished draughtsman. His design for the completion of St. Petronio at Bologna is beautifully drawn, and is technically superior to any of the drawings in that most interesting collection, though it is inferior in interest to the strange design by Baldassare Peruzzi and the diagram drawings of Terribilia.* In spite of Palladio's undoubted ability and pre-eminent success, I incline to think that he was at least as intent on his public as on his art. Good man as he was, he was

---

* The drawings for the completion of St. Petronio are now in the museum of that church. According to the author of the catalogue (M. Angelo Gatti, Bologna, 1894), the basis of the collection was formed by Terribilia about the year 1570. It now contains some fifty-one designs and a wood model of the church dating from the sixteenth century. The most important of the designs are those made by Peruzzi between 1522–23, Vignola about 1547, Giulio Romano and C. Lombard (1546), Ranuzzi (1547) ; a design by Dominique de Varignana, which was actually begun in 1556 ; Terribilia's designs and diagrams ; designs by Palladio (1577–79) ; and by Rainaldi (1626).

content with rather cheap and easy attainments, stucco instead of masonry in his architecture, conventions instead of searching study in his drawings ; and one will look in vain in his works for anything like such a drawing as this plate of the Composite order which I reproduce from the rare first edition of Vignola's *Regola delle Cinque Ordini*, dedicated to Cardinal Farnese, and issued, I believe, at about the same date as Palladio's *Architettura*.

The examples illustrated are typical of the methods of illustrating books on architecture, in use in Italy throughout the sixteenth century. The two illustrations from the title pages of Barbaro's *Vitruvius*, published by Marcolini (1556), and Palladio's *Architettura*, published by Domenico Franceschi of Venice (1570), show how far they could go. It is not first-rate work, but it has the merit of simplicity of statement, and its technical superiority is evident on a comparison with the illustrations of De l'Orme's *Architecture* of about the same date. De l'Orme was an artist of much ability and energy, but uncertain in taste, and a somewhat unscrupulous poacher. On p. 256, *verso*, in Chaudière's * edition, is an illustration of a frontispiece with two lofty obelisks at the end, lifted bodily from Serlio's fourth book (Plate LVIII., Venetian edition of 1551). One of his drawings of an Ionic capital, which he says he measured himself from the antique, has a suspicious resemblance to a drawing by Antonio da San Gallo the elder in the Uffizi collection. De l'Orme's perspective view of the Chapel of Anet is out of drawing, so is the absurdly designed house on p. 254, *verso*, and the man who could do so badly as this would hardly have made the excellent sectional perspective of the Colosseum on the opposite page, a drawing which was probably annexed by De l'Orme from some Italian. There are other examples scattered up and down his book of the same sort, but there is also much that is original and authentic : his diagrams

* Paris, 1626, Regnauld Chaudière.

I DIECI LIBRI.
DELL'ARCHITETTVRA DI M.
VITRVVIO TRADVTTI ET
COMMENTATI DA MONSIGNOR
BARBARO ELETTO PATRIARCA
D'AQVILEGGIA.

Con due Tauole, l'una di tutto quello si contiene per i
Capi nell'Opera, l'altra per dichiaratione di tutte
le cose d'importanza.

IN VINEGIA, PER FRANCESCO MARCOLINI CON PRIVILEGGI. M D LVI.

Frontispiece of Daniele Barbaro's Edition of *Vitruvius* (Venice, 1556)

The Frontispiece of the *Architettura* of Andrea Palladio (1570)

of stereotomy, his details of carpentry, his famous "good and bad architects," and the characteristic drawing of a Corinthian Triumphal Arch (Bk. VIII. 245), which he says was converted from a triumph to a "*grandissime désolation et désastre*," the fate of most of poor De l'Orme's schemes in his latter days. The drawing of part of the construction of a roof (p. 292) shows De l'Orme at his best, and is an excellent example of a detail perfectly understood and clearly represented. (See facing p. 27.)

I have referred to De l'Orme more on account of the historical interest of his illustrations than for their value as drawings, but meanwhile France had produced an architectural draughtsman pure and simple, without parallel either in England or in Italy. The Italians had their own way of drawing architecture—a method, as will be seen from the illustrations from Serlio and Palladio, that rather glided over difficulties of detail, but was well adapted for showing the general idea of a building in the most direct way. These men used a firm, thick line, suitable for the wood-block, and though, as in the case of Serlio, they employed perspective on occasion, it was perspective of a rudimentary sort, and their drawings were diagrams rather than illustrations. In 1575 Etienne du Perac produced his *Vestigi dell' Antiquita di Roma*, a rare book containing some thirty-nine freehand sketches engraved on copper. Du Perac's work has considerable archæological value to this day. His object was, as he says in his dedication, "*rappresentar fidelmente i residui della Romana grandezza*," and this he did with much greater loyalty than Palladio. But neither he nor the Italians seem to have satisfied the French instinct for completeness, and the next advance in architectural drawing was due to Jacques Androuet du Cerceau, that indefatigable draughtsman who spent his life in turning out worthless architectural fancies and fragments that did more harm than good, and also in making views of the great houses of France, which are of inestimable value.

I have elsewhere * described Du Cerceau's position as an artist, and shall merely sum up the conclusion I came to—that on the one hand he had little genuine sense of architecture, and that as a designer of multifarious detail he was almost wholly mischievous, but that, on the other hand, the work that he did in his *Plus Excellents Bastimens* is quite admirable in its way, and of the highest value to the historical student. One has only to compare them with Thorpe's drawings to realise the importance of the work done by the Frenchman.

Du Cerceau's technique was curious and, in a way, limited. He had at his command a line of unfaltering precision ; the splendid series of drawings in the British Museum show that he could, if he wished, draw almost anything. On the other hand, there is little trace of an imagination reaching beyond the subject, and giving hints of alluring possibilities, such as is found in the thumb-nail sketches of Peruzzi and the younger San Gallo. His drawings are very clear and of scientific accuracy, but they leave one cold ; they are tight, if one may say so of a drawing, unsuggestive, unresponsive. Du Cerceau worked conscientiously at his versions of buildings, indifferent apparently to anything but the exact statement of the building as it was. He seems to have been intensely honest in these drawings of buildings, and the opposite in his fancy designs. And it is on the former that his enduring reputation rests. The other half of his work raises the whole question of the draughtsman-designer ; that is, of the man who sits at his drawing-board, and turns out design after design without regard to materials, and to the conditions of their realisation in fact. There was an unwholesome growth of such men at the end of the sixteenth century : Du Cerceau *par excellence*, followed by the Flemings or Germans, Wendel Dietterlin † and De Vries,‡ with their tedious

* *History of French Architecture*, 1494–1661 (Bell & Sons), Vol. I, pp. 147–150.

† *De Quinque Columnarum Simmetrica Distributione*, per Vindelinum Dieterlin, Pictorem argentinensem, 1593.   ‡ Vriese, or De Vries, published his book of designs in 1563.

ingenuity and deplorable taste, and in a different manner by Sambin,* of Dijon, a better draughtsman, but ambitious and vulgar.

These men were the forerunners of the much more considerable draughtsmen of the seventeenth century whom I shall discuss in the next chapter. They are all members of the same family, industrious builders of *châteaux d'Espagne*, indefatigable and unprofitable designers in the air. Du Cerceau was a draughtsman, Sambin a carver, Dietterlin a painter. Instead of approaching architecture from the point of view of planning and construction, of proportion and scale, they treated the art as free material for every conceivable freak and caprice of ornament. It is possible that these plates may now and then suggest ideas. Personally, when looking through these books of design, from Du Cerceau down to Oppenord, I have never found the thing I wanted, the exact phrase for the idea one wished to convey. That there has always been a market for such work is shown by the abundance of these books of design in the seventeenth and eighteenth centuries. Yet it seems to me almost impossible that, in a design thought out from end to end, a design that aims at unity of effect, these gobbets from another mind can be rightly assimilated; they can only result in a compilation of architectural details without meaning or cohesion. The point of view of such men is widely removed from that of the architect. The latter has to design under specific conditions. The scale and character of his chimneypiece, for example, is conditioned by the scale and character of the room in which it stands, and it is not till he has these data as a point of departure that flint and steel meet, as it were, and that his mind can begin to work to any purpose on the problem before him. But the draughtsman of the type of Du Cerceau,

---

* *Œuvre de la Diversité des Termes, etc.*, par Maistre Hugues Sambin, demeurant à Dijon. Lyons, 1572. A collection of designs of terminal figures, many of them of the most appalling description.

F

the ornamentalist, is like the spider who spins his net anywhere and everywhere for the unwary; moreover, he has, more often than not, been caught in his own net, and been deceived by the facility of his own pencil. Those curves and volutes and fancy foliage were well enough in the drawn line, but quite another thing translated into some intractable material; and it is here, in this disregard of material and handicraft, that the work of many of these draughtsmen and engravers has been so dangerous to the Arts.

Here is a plate from De Vries engraved in 1563, and one from the book that Dietterlin dedicated " *nobili et ornatissimo viro Conrad Schlosberger* " in 1593. I only show these plates in order that the student may know what to avoid. Either of these plates or any one of Sambin's " Termes " is an epitome of all that is vile and abominable in design. Yet Dietterlin believed it to be serious architecture. He dedicated his work to amateurs, and " the ruder mechanics," as he calls the unfortunate workmen who were to carry out his designs, and believed he was doing service to the Art. Sambin describes one of his " Termes " as composed after the five orders of the antique, and as " *simple en enrichissement, bien proportionné.* "

The havoc that such men wrought in German and Flemish and in our own Elizabethan and Jacobean art is well known to students. When architectural draughtsmen launched out into such stuff as this, there was no reason why they should ever stop. Men of the type of De Vries and Dietterlin, and even Du Cerceau, considered as ornamentalists, are the parasites of architecture, whom students should entirely eschew. The aim of the student should be first-hand knowledge acquired by study and observation; knowledge of the ends to be aimed at in art; knowledge of the methods and materials through which those ends are to be realised. The draughtsman's line should be the expression of

Sheet of Details. By De Vries (1563)

A Design by Wendel Dietterlin (1593)

this knowledge, its means of conveyance to other minds and other hands ; and unless there is this knowledge behind the drawing, inspiring and controlling it, the results will be disastrous. To architects most of all, draughtsmanship, essential as it is, must play the part of a servant, not of a master ; it is not there for the display of virtuosity, but for the serious and considered statement of knowledge and thought. And it is this that to some extent differentiates the purpose of architectural draughtsmanship from the drawing of the free artist. The latter might find some quality of colour or form that it might be worth his while to interpret for certain purposes in buildings or figures of the most repulsive description. But to the architectural draughtsman the content of what he is drawing is a matter of vital importance ; indeed, it is to convey it to others that his drawing is made, and his hand should therefore be guided and restrained by knowledge of the purpose of his design and of the conditions under which it is to be carried out.—I am referring, of course, to drawings made by designers, not to views of buildings made as illustrations, a branch of architectural draughtsmanship to some extent on common ground with that of the painter.

The relations of draughtsmanship to architectural design have often been misunderstood. There have been times when the designing of architecture has meant little more than the power of architectural drawing and a pretty thorough knowledge of the orders. In recent years the balance has swung to the opposite extreme. Because construction is of essential importance in architectural design, men have been tempted to say that draughtsmanship does not matter. That view I believe to be as mistaken as the other. Draughtsmanship is certainly not architecture, but the architect's business is not merely to state the facts of construction in his building ; he has to state them in a form that is beautiful, and it is difficult to see how, as an artist, he is to arrive at those forms simply by internal meditation and without the aids and resources that draughtsmanship can supply in working out his ideas and giving them their final shape. At the bottom of bad draughtsmanship lie imperfect powers of observation ; the eye has not been sufficiently trained to become sensitive to refinements of form and to subtle relations of proportion, a faculty which is essential to fine architectural design. The constant study of form is quite as important for the architect as it is for the sculptor, and the readiest means of qualifying oneself to visualise form, to realise it and render it intelligible to others, is the study of drawing. Architectural students have to learn to observe accurately and closely, and this is the reason why trick drawing and merely conventional statements of objects seen are worse than useless. That habit, if persisted in, ends by depriving the draughtsman of the power of seeing things as they actually are, because he gets into the habit of regarding the objects that he sees not as so much fresh material for study and realisation, but merely an occasion for trotting out one of his stock of pet conventions. Harding's trees and Prout's buildings are the result. The remedy is the searching study of form. The men of fifty years ago—Burges, for example—used to urge strongly the necessity of figure drawing for the architectural student, and I think they were perfectly right. There should be no unnecessary barriers between the idea and its realisation, and one immediate obstacle can at any rate be removed by the tenacious and intelligent study of draughtsmanship.

Plate IX. *Livre d'Architecture.* By Alexander Francini (1640)

Designs for Panels. Drawn by Jean Lepautre. Engraved by Le Blond

CHAPTER III

DU CERCEAU founded two traditions of architectural draughtsmanship in France : the first, that of details of design for every sort of decoration ; the second, and far more valuable one, that of the accurate record of existing buildings. Du Cerceau himself had run riot in all sorts of caprices, and nothing came amiss to his untiring pencil—candlesticks, cabinets, jewellery, metalwork, grotesques, arabesques, houses, temples, subjects from religion and mythology—he dealt with all, with impartial and undeviating bad taste. His successors in France were rather more cautious, and, for a time, produced collections of designs for special arts and handicrafts, such as the treatise on ironwork issued by Matthurin Jousse of La Flèche, in 1625, a work prepared with some regard to the actual processes of the metal-worker. Matthurin Jousse was blacksmith to the Jesuits of La Flèche, and was helped by Martellange, the Jesuit architect, in the preparation of his books.* Of Barbet and Collot, who both issued collections of architectural details a few years later, very little is known. Barbet dedicated a book of altars and chimney-pieces to Richelieu, engraved by Abraham Bosse, in 1635. His illustrations are of interest because, according to his own account, they were drawn from recent examples in Paris, and so represent the details of

---

* Matthurin Jousse was a remarkable man in his way, for he also published a translation of Viator's *Perspective* in 1626, a treatise on carpentry, and a treatise on the five orders, and in 1642 a book on stereotomy entitled *Le Secret d'Architecture, découvrant fidèlement les traits géométriques."* See Destailleur's *Notices sur Quelques Artistes Français,* pp. 52–54.

domestic architecture in the little-studied period of the reign of Louis XIII. Collot's work, though different in manner, belongs to the same period. Both men were contemporaries of Le Muet, the well-known architect, and of Francini, the engraver and water-engineer of Florence. Francini's designs of doorways according to the five orders are in the taste of the worst designs of the time of Louis XIII., and in no sense representative of the best work of a period which has been little studied and imperfectly understood by modern students. The one which is reproduced (facing p. 36, Plate IX.) is the least offensive of a bad lot, but it is only fair to Francini to mention that in his preface he disclaims any qualification for his work but the amiable, if inadequate, merit of a sincere admiration for architecture as the first of the arts.

Pierre Le Muet, on the other hand, was an able architect. His *Manière de bien Bastir* was the first serious attempt to deal with domestic architecture since the days of De l'Orme's colossal undertaking. The plates are well drawn and well engraved, and students in studying the work of Le Muet should be careful to do so in the original edition, and not in the abominable reprint that Jombert published in the eighteenth century, for Jombert was one of those publishing pirates who collected plates of all kinds and dates, touched them up and usually spoilt them, and then reissued them as new publications. Le Muet's work suffered more than most of them at his hands. Plate I. of the second part in the edition of 1647 is a characteristic example of Le Muet's method, and shows the difference between the work of the trained architect and the casual designer such as Francini. Abraham Bosse, the draughtsman and engraver, a capable but very quarrelsome artist, published his treatise on the drawing of the five orders in 1664,* a finely engraved folio containing many plates of details of the orders, and some geometrical designs of doorways which

---

* A second edition was issued in 1688, in which the dedication to Colbert is omitted.

Designs for a Frieze. By Jean Lepautre

Designs for Arabesques. Drawn by Jean Lepautre. Engraved by Mariette

represent the dying tradition of François Mansart and Le Muet. Bosse dedicated his work to Colbert ; but that far-seeing Minister was already on the look out for younger and more imaginative draughtsmen, and the interminable undertaking of the *Cabinet du Roi* was already started.

Of this new generation of draughtsmen and designers the most important figure in France in the third quarter of the seventeenth century was Jean Lepautre, brother of the well-known architect, Antoine Lepautre, an artist who shares with Daniel Marot the distinction of being the most prolific and the most brilliant draughtsman of the seventeenth century. Jean Lepautre was born in 1617, and was apprenticed to a cabinet-maker in Paris named Adam Philippon, a man of considerable intelligence, who had been employed under Louis XIII. as an agent in Rome to collect antiques and to engage skilled Italian workmen for the French Court. Destailleur suggests that Philippon took young Lepautre with him to Rome and employed him to make the drawings of details which he published himself in 1645.* No artist in France in 1645 could consider himself a master of his art unless he had studied in Rome, and the story is intrinsically probable ; but with Lepautre, except for a certain parade of the ordinary classical paraphernalia, the Roman influence was only skin-deep. Lepautre was essentially a Frenchman, and as much a Frenchman of his period as Du Cerceau had been of his. His first published work was issued in 1644, and for a time he devoted himself to the reproduction of pictures by various masters. His first efforts to get out of the rut were not very happy. During the *Fronde* he got into trouble through a caricature of Mazarin, representing Mlle. de Montpensier sweeping the cardinal out of France with a broom, and on the plate was a very injurious inscription. The cardinal, however, forgave him, with characteristic

* Destailleur, *Notices*, etc., p. 68–69.

irony, and Lepautre atoned for the error of his ways by engravings of unimpeachable loyalty to the throne. His real interest as an artist begins with his amazing sets of designs for decorations, of which the earliest known example is dated 1657.* He produced design after design for every conceivable decoration—interiors, chimney-pieces, ceilings, alcoves, cartouches, mausolea, grottoes, fountains, and vases—the series seem inexhaustible. Mariette says that Lepautre hardly took the trouble to make any preliminary studies, but began straight away on the copper, improvising as he went ; and this quality is, I think, characteristic of Lepautre. His mind must have worked with extraordinary rapidity. There is little trace of profound study in his work, and no affectation whatever of archæological research. In his ceilings, for example, he adopted off-hand the general arrangement of ribs and compartments customary at the time. But given that as a datum, his fancy began to play on it with a richness and facility that recalls to some extent the exuberant genius of Rubens. Its charm is its obvious wealth of resource, its never-failing ease and vivacity, and a certain gallant manner, so different and so refreshing after the laboured banalities of Du Cerceau. It was the true expression of those splendid opening years of the reign of Louis XIV.

In 1668 Lepautre was employed by the Court to engrave the fêtes of Versailles, and in the following year to engrave the audience given by Louis XIV. to Soloman Aga Mustapha Feraga, the ambassador of the Sultan. In 1670, Colbert entrusted him

* In 1654 Lepautre had already designed and engraved some of those pictures, set in elaborate borders, of which there are many examples in his later work. The 1654 set was sold by J. Van Merlen in the Rue St. Jacques, Antwerp, as appears on a title page in my collection. It should be noted that Lepautre did not always engrave his own drawings. Le Blond, Pierre Mariette, and Langlois engraved them on occasion, and the student should again regard with suspicion Jombert's reprints of 1751. Jean Le Blond was uncle of the Jean Baptiste Alexandre Le Blond, painter and architect, who illustrated, if he did not write, the *Théorie et Pratique du Jardinage* in 1709, and was an excellent draughtsman.

Design for a Chimneypiece. Drawn by Jean Lepautre.
Engraved by Le Blond

Vase. By Jean Lepautre

Vase. By Jean Lepautre

with part of the engravings made for the *Cabinet du Roi*,* that famous series of engravings which was to include all the notable features of the reign of Louis XIV., and did actually extend to twenty-three folio volumes. Lepautre drew and engraved views of the grotto at Versailles in the years 1672-3-6, and in the latter year he produced plates of the performance of *Alcestis* in the Cour de Marbre and of the *Malade Imaginaire* in the gardens before the grotto, and some remarkable illustrations of the fireworks and illuminations at Versailles. But Lepautre was not at his best in the *Cabinet du Roi*. He may have been frightened by the insistent interference of Colbert ; his work here is timid and uncertain, and has little of the verve and brilliancy that he shows elsewhere. Indeed, it must have been difficult for any artist of strong individuality to do himself justice in the service of Colbert and the King, and under the ponderous control of such men as Le Brun and J. H. Mansart. However, the work that Lepautre did for Colbert carried him into the Academy of Painting and Sculpture, and established his reputation as the leading engraver of his day. He continued to turn out plate after plate almost up to the day of his death in 1682. His industry was prodigious, and only equalled by his amazing facility of design and draughtsmanship. Destailleur estimates that he engraved at least two thousand plates as against some thirteen to fourteen hundred by Du Cerceau ; and in addition he must have made sketches innumerable for every sort of purpose. His record has been beaten by Hollar alone, who produced over 2,700 engraved plates in some fifty years, and even Piranesi falls short of him in quantity, though it must be borne in mind that many of Piranesi's plates were very elaborate and very much larger.

* There is an incomplete copy of this in the library of the Royal Institute of British Architects. Vol. XXIII. is missing. The original copper plates are still in existence.

G

Lepautre issued interminable series of sets of small engravings, alcoves *à l'Italienne et à la Romaine*, designs for panels, friezes, vases, mausolea, chapels, screens, grotesques, ceilings, cartouches, candelabra, and scenes from the "Metamorphoses" of Ovid, according to the accepted versions of classical subjects as handled by Le Brun and the Romanised French painters of the time. Architecture, figures, and landscapes were all handled in turn, and again and again ; for, in spite of the abundance of his work, the area of his artistic thought lay in a rather small compass. His figure subjects were mainly variations on themes supplied by the school of the Carracci ; that is, they were competent, but conventional and unconvincing. His architecture was based on Louis Le Vau rather than on François Mansart ; and his detail of ornament was exuberant and unrestrained. It is not here that his originality is to be sought. Lepautre was too facile in conception and execution to be capable of striking out one of those great imaginative designs which hold the mind as something beyond the reach of other men—such a design as that plate by Bramante to which I have already referred. Where he was strong, and perhaps unsurpassed by anyone, was in his power of presentation. His imagination was essentially dramatic, as, indeed, was the age in which he lived—that age of Louis XIV., in which half men's lives were spent in ceremonial and nearly all of it in play-acting. Lepautre was quick to seize on features which would at once arrest attention—violent action, richness and audacity of ornament, and he could combine his motives with a freshness of invention and brilliancy of draughtsmanship such as few men have ever possessed. His vases for gardens, for example, are very much more than mere working drawings of a vase. They are, as it were, the heroic type and embodiment of all vases, as Lepautre conceived of them, magnificent in ornament, splendid in position, amid the environment of the most glorious Court in

Namur. By Pierre Lepautre (after 1692). From the *Cabinet du Roi*

Besançon. By Daniel Marot. From the *Cabinet du Roi*

the world. Working only in black and white, he has yet contrived to invest them with an atmosphere of their own, suggesting their association with stately architecture, the play of light and shade on their ornament, the wind in the trees behind them, and the cloud and sunshine in the sky. The small frontispiece to a series of vases, with *amorini* supporting the inscription, and a background of terraces and architecture, is inimitable in its suggestiveness. So, though perhaps in a somewhat more flamboyant manner, is the great vase from the larger series; for Lepautre, so far from using his purple patch with discretion, in point of fact scarcely ever used anything else, and though he was continually drawing architecture, his thought never shaped itself in architecture : he could only think and clothe his thought in terms of ornament. In this he is the exact opposite of Piranesi ; but, on the other hand, his ornament was exceedingly fine in its way, large in scale, and conceived of on a great decorative plan, and it carries with it a suggestion of atmosphere and environment scarcely to be found in the work of any other man.

I have criticised Du Cerceau's work as an ornamentalist unfavourably, as remote from the conditions of execution, and as unreasonable and trivial in itself. Lepautre also produced designs regardless of the difficulties of material and workmanship, probably with a sublime confidence in the skill of his countrymen, or much more probably as simple fantasies of his imagination—dreams and visions of what might be in a world that never could exist. But there is a notable difference between the work of Lepautre and the work of Du Cerceau. Where the latter was trifling in scale, and laboured with a fancy that never rose above the *mesquineries* of ornament, the imagination of Lepautre ranged far and wide. His schemes of decoration were organic in the sense that he aimed at a large unity of effect, in which each detail of his ornament was subordinated to the whole. It is here that he is so far superior not only to Du Cerceau before him, but to Berain, who succeeded him. Berain, too, was a skilful artist, dexterous with his needle and a master of Court pageants, but his imagination never soared into the empyrean. Lepautre was indeed one of the most remarkable among the French artists of the seventeenth century. Bernini, a fine judge, who had no great reason to love the French, thought highly of his work, and his influence on French architectural decoration lasted into the eighteenth century; indeed, it has been fully appreciated by all French artists except the pedants and poseurs of the Revolution and the First Empire. Destailleur gives the curious information that in the eighteenth century a complete set of his works was worth from 130 to 150 francs. In 1827 they sold for 30 francs. I do not know what they would be worth now, but probably not less than 1,500 francs; and it is such a case as this that induces caution in accepting reputations unless verified by the verdict of time. From the historical point of view, the work of Lepautre is important, because it gives full expression to that mature art which the labours of generations of Frenchmen had built up, and which reached its culminating point in the reign of Louis XIV. The wide difference that separates the work of Lepautre from that of Du Cerceau was not solely due to the genius of Lepautre. It was also a striking testimony to the advance that French art had made in the hundred years which separate the death of Jean Lepautre from that of Jacques Androuet du Cerceau.

The Lepautre, as the Du Cerceau, were a family of artists. Pierre Lepautre, the eldest son of Jean, helped his father in his latter days, and after his death was employed by Jules Hardouin Mansart to engrave many of the royal buildings, and in private, perhaps, to act as ghost to that extremely astute and not very scrupulous architect. Mariette makes the significant remark that Mansart employed the younger Lepautre "*pour rédiger et mestre*

Design for a Ceiling. By Daniel Marot

Design for a Ceiling.　By Daniel Marot

au net ses pensées," and adds that, in fact, Lepautre made nearly all the drawings for the buildings and gardens at Versailles, Marly, and the royal houses. It was not for nothing that Jules Hardouin Mansart was " *surintendant des Bâtiments,"* King's Counsellor, and Chevalier of the Order of St. Michel, drawing in salaries 50,000 livres per annum. It is only fair to add that he managed to get a special post created for Pierre Lepautre, viz. that of draughtsman and engraver of the royal buildings. Pierre Lepautre was, in fact, a most capable draughtsman. To the *Cabinet du Roi* he contributed, among other drawings, a fine bird's-eye view of the Invalides, and an excellent engraving of Namur made after its capture in 1692 (facing p. 42). He is believed to have died in 1716.

Meanwhile, another most able draughtsman had been coming to the front. Daniel Marot was the son of Jean Marot, the architect, to whose work I shall return later, and was born in 1650. He began his training in the excellent school of his father, from whom he learnt a precision in architectural design in which Lepautre had been lacking ; but the influence of the latter was irresistible, and the work of Daniel Marot came to resemble so closely that of Lepautre that, except for the signatures, it would be difficult in certain cases to tell the work of one from the other. The work that he did for the *Cabinet du Roi* is some of the best in the entire collection. There is a very clear and precise perspective of the Invalides, and the plates of Maestricht, Dôle, Besançon, and Yprès are masterpieces of black and white in line, both in design and execution.* I reproduce the plate of Besançon (facing p. 43) to show how attractive this kind of illustration can become in really competent hands. Daniel Marot was gaining a foremost place among French draughtsmen when his career was abruptly checked by the iniquitous Revocation of the Edict of Nantes, which cost France some of the ablest of her sons—soldiers, merchants,

* Vol. XX., *Cabinet du Roi.*

artists, and craftsmen of all sorts. Marot, as a Protestant, had to
fly the country, and took refuge in Holland, where he entered the
service of Louis' most inveterate enemy, William of Orange, our
William III., and at the Dutch Court spent the rest of his life in
multifarious designs of decorations, gardens, and, more rarely,
architecture. The great majority of his published engravings
were made in Holland.* He usually described himself as " Architect to the King of Great Britain." The only work in England
said to have been designed by Marot was one of the parterres at
Hampton Court. Among many other designs that he made in
Holland is one of the magnificent state carriage built at The
Hague in 1698, in point of execution an inimitable piece of
engraving.

Marot made it his business to supply "*pensées*," as he called them,
for architects, painters, sculptors, jewellers, gardeners, and others.
In other words, his books were pattern books, naked and un-
ashamed. If, as appears to be the case, there is no escaping these
parasites of modern architecture, one could only wish they were
up to the standard of Marot and Lepautre. Such was the brilliancy of Marot's drawing that, as in the case of his master, many
of his engravings are works of art in themselves, of great beauty,
and some of his ceilings are finer than almost anything by Lepautre.
Two examples are here illustrated. Properly executed, how magnificent these might have been with Marot to set out the ceiling
and some colourist of genius to deal with the figures of the
central panels. Tiepolo himself could not have conveyed more
admirably the sense of space and the joy of the open sky ; but
Tiepolo (born in 1693) was probably not born when Marot made
these drawings. The exact date when they were made is not
known. The engravings were made after Marot left France, as the

* All the engravings reproduced by Wasmuth (Berlin, 1892) date from the Holland
period. Daniel Marot is last heard of in 1718, having been born in 1650.

Design for a State Coach. By Daniel Marot

A Design for Decoration. By Berain

inscription on the plates says, "*avec privilege des États généraux des provinces unies*," but I incline to think they were made while he was still under the influence of Lepautre, for his manner altered, not entirely for the good, in Holland. It may have been, as Destailleur suggests, that the dull air of Holland deadened his wits, but it is impossible to accept entirely the view of that distinguished writer that Daniel Marot was a lost leader, the superior of Lepautre, and one of the most accomplished artists ever produced by France. Marot was a very clever and dexterous artist, and, as these ceilings show, had he been given a fair chance, might have gone far. But Fate was against him. He had to limit his imagination and his engravings to the domestic details of Holland. He lost touch of the grand manner of Louis XIV., and became rather trivial and even commonplace. His drawings of urns, for example, are poor things after those inventions of Lepautre, instinct with the romance and pageantry of a great Court life. Nor had he the inexhaustible vitality of Lepautre, that never-failing resource and invention in the combination of figures with architectural features. But he was most skilful in the design of minor ornament, with more sense of style than Berain and more solidity of taste than Meissonnier. Lepautre and Daniel Marot were perhaps the finest masters of decorative draughtsmanship that have ever existed, and in saying this I do not for an instant place them in competition with the Italian painters who have imagined and carried out great schemes of decorative painting. The Frenchmen are, of course, upon a lower plane, but both of them had something of the quality that Tiepolo possessed in a consummate degree ; as improvisatori in ornament these two men were inimitable.

Jean Berain was born about the middle of the seventeenth century in Lorraine, the country of Callot and Sylvestre, and is supposed to have died in 1711 or 1722. He was an important man at the French Court, being draughtsman of the

Cabinet du Roi,* with a lodging below the Grand Gallery in the Louvre. On the death of Israel Sylvestre in 1691 he succeeded to his rooms. Mariette says that he gave the designs for all the scenery and dresses for the Opera at Paris, and for all the plays and ceremonies of the Court. Berain acquired a considerable reputation for little quips and cranks of design, which came to be known as " Berinades "—monkeys swinging very fat babies, satyrs piping arm in arm, creatures ending in consoles, set out in a fanciful background of curves and volutes from which hang flower-pots and garlands, with parrots and other strange-looking birds perched about the design. His designs for chimney-pieces, which he dedicated to Mansart, are not attractive, but would, no doubt, have been redeemed by the splendid workmanship of their execution. Berain was at his best in his designs for the surface of walls and ceilings, and in spite of their frivolity, or perhaps because of it, there is a good deal of charm in these fantastic decorations, which in certain particulars remind one of Du Cerceau, but possess a vivacity and movement lacking in the latter. Berain was an extremely skilful engraver, and his plates of metal-work are masterpieces in their way.

I now turn to the other side of French architectural draughtsmanship, the record of existing buildings. It was a less ambitious aim than that of the artists we have been discussing, but the work done by such men as Du Cerceau in the sixteenth century, and Jean Marot, Israel Sylvestre, and the Perelle in the seventeenth, is of far greater value to the historical student. Israel Sylvestre engraved a number of plates of Versailles, the Louvre, and the Tuileries, in Vols. XI., XIV., and XVII. of the *Cabinet du Roi*, and views of Chambord, St. Germain, Monceaux, and Fontainebleau in Vol. XVII., and he was widely employed as a draughtsman.

* Berain, with Chauveau and Le Moine, engraved the ornaments and decorations of the Tuileries and the Louvre in Vol. XVII. of the *Cabinet du Roi*, about 1710.

Designs for Escutcheons by Brisuile.   Engraved by Jean Berain

Arc de Triomphe dressé   dans le marché neuf

A Triumphal Arch. By Jean Marot. Figures probably by Daniel Marot

But his work is less accomplished than that of Perelle, who drew the landscape in several of the battle plates in Vol. VII. of the *Cabinet du Roi*, and divides with Jean Marot the honour of being the first topographical draughtsman of France. Jean Marot was the father of Daniel and of a son, Jean, who appears to have helped in his work and, according to Destailleur, has been confused with him. Jean Marot, the father, was an architect of ability. His design for the completion of the Louvre is at least as good as Lemercier's, and he designed some considerable houses and the Church of the Feuillantines in Paris. He also made and engraved various projects or designs in the air, all of which show a certain sobriety and precision learnt from actual experience of building; but his really valuable work is his *Architecture Française* (195 plates), known as the *Grand Marot*, and the little folio, containing 112 geometrical drawings of notable buildings of the time, known as the *Petit Marot*, one of the most perfect little books of its kind in existence.*

I give three characteristic examples of his drawings. These drawings perhaps show Jean Marot at his best. As an accurate geometrical draughtsman of architecture he was excellent, but his perspectives, though he perfectly well understood the rules, are rather lifeless, and Jean Marot was a poor hand at the figure, and unless he was helped by Lepautre or La Bella, his figures are bad, if not ridiculous. In the fine plate which I reproduce and which is signed " Jean Marot, *fecit*," all the figures and the panel, and enrichments above the main entablature, were almost certainly drawn by Daniel Marot on architecture set up by his father. Jean Marot drew too much as an architect, and not enough as a painter; that is, in his anxiety for accuracy he

---

* In regard to this latter book I should point out that the quality of the engravings is lost in any enlargements, which simply ruin the delicacy of their draughtsmanship.

H

sometimes missed the essential elements of the design and gave a
wrong impression of the building.

Such drawings as the view of Chambord, by one of the
Perelle, with its cavalcade of horsemen, were beyond the reach
of Marot, and I know no illustration, certainly no photograph,
which gives anything like so vivid and correct an impression of
Chambord, of its bizarre outline, of that sentiment of François I.
that still broods over its roofs, of the loneliness of this strange
jewel set in the desolate woodlands of the Sologne. To the Perelle,
moreover, we owe a new departure in architectural drawing, and
that is the perspective with the sight line high up in the picture,
the great bird's-eye view of houses and grounds stretching away
for miles into the country. Du Cerceau had made bird's-eye views,
beautifully drawn as far as they went, such as Gaillon and Blois,
but they were unimaginative outline drawings, such as a surveyor
or an engineer might make if he could draw as well as Du
Cerceau. The buildings might stand in the plain or on the moun-
tain, amid rocks or in the middle of a ploughed field, for all one
can learn from Du Cerceau's drawings ; but on Perelle's bird's-
eye views there is that same suggestion of atmosphere which
I have already noted in another way as pre-eminent in some
of the drawings of Lepautre. Nor was this power obtained
by any rigid convention of draughtsmanship. In his plates of
Maisons, or Liencour, Perelle suggests the ideals of the time of
Mazarin and Anne of Austria, not less clearly than he had indicated those of François I. at Chambord, the ordered sobriety of
design which separates the age of François Mansart from the
caprice and experiment of the amateur of the early Renaissance.

Israel Sylvestre and the Perelle, father and sons,* approached

* It is by no means easy to differentiate between the work of the Perelle.' Gabriel
Perelle, the father, was born at Vernon early in the seventeenth century, and was a
pupil of a certain Daniel Rabel, a painter ; he helped Sylvestre with his work, both as a

Lemercier's Entrance to the Louvre. By Jean Marot

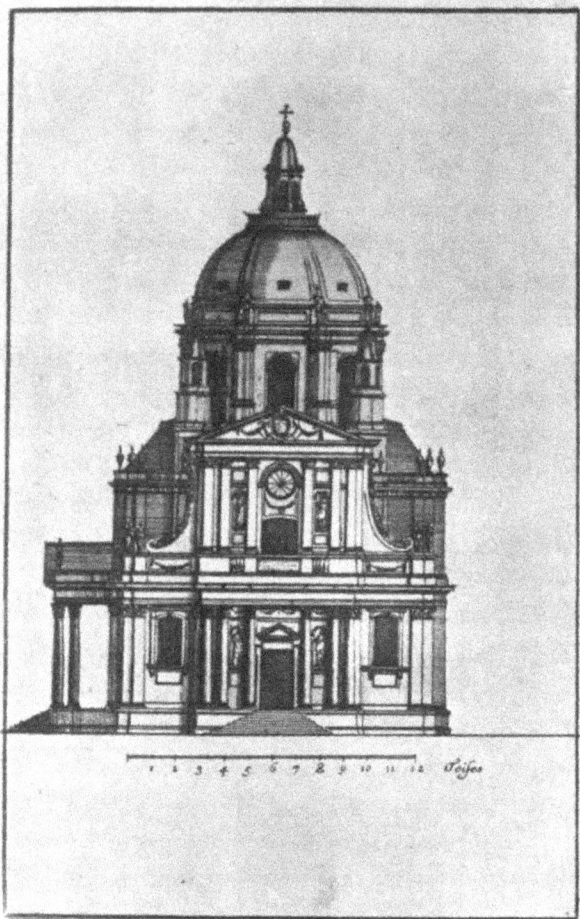

Le grand portail de l'Eglise de la Sorbonne du costé de la rue.

The Sorbonne. By Jean Marot. From the *Petit Marot*

architectural drawing from a point of view widely removed from that of Du Cerceau. Sylvestre came from that school of Nancy, in Lorraine, which had produced Jaques Callot, and his training in drawing, and that of the Perelle, must have been more complete than that of Du Cerceau or Jean Marot, for their figures are almost as good as those of Callot himself, and their power of drawing landscape and architecture considerably better. Moreover, they had a sense of composition, wanting in the drawings of Du Cerceau and Marot. It is a difficult thing to make a complete and satisfactory bird's-eye view. In a sumptuous volume on gardens, recently brought out in France, there are some attempts at bird's-eye views of modern gardens which fail in the most lamentable manner, in the first place because what design there is is meagre and inadequate, and in the second place because the draughtsman has not even thought out the design, such as it is, but has concealed part of it with clumsy foregrounds and let the rest lose itself in a meaningless and unnecessary haze. Such drawings as those of the Perelle (father and sons) mean not only complete technical accomplishment of hand, but systematic and sustained thought, and considerable power of visualisation; they are an excellent corrective to those merely impressionistic sketches of modern artists which too often mask incompetence to carry the drawing further.

The fashion set by these great French topographical draughtsmen extended to England. They inspired the well-known views of English houses drawn by Knyff, and engraved by Kip, which appeared in 1709 with the title of *Britannia Illustrata*, and the plates that Kip and others engraved for Atkyn's *Gloucestershire*

teacher and as a draughtsman, and he appears to be the Perelle whose name appears in certain of the engravings of the *Cabinet du Roi*, notably on the battle and siege views engraved under the direction of Beaulieu, the engineer. Gabriel, who died in 1675, had two sons, Nicolas and Adam, excellent draughtsmen and engravers, whose work is hardly distinguishable from that of their father. *See* Mariette, Abecedario, "*Perelle.*"

and similar books. A comparison of Kip's engraving with almost any plate by the Perelle will, however, show the incontestable superiority of the latter, not only in technique as draughtsmen and engravers, but in their imaginative grasp of the problem. The arts were more vital in France in the latter part of the seventeenth century than they had yet become in England. We had as yet—that is, before the rise of Wren—produced only one architect of first-rate ability in Inigo Jones, an artist who, apart from his genius for architecture, produced in his designs for the scenery of masques drawings not unworthy of Lepautre himself, and architectural drawings not inferior to the work of those sixteenth century Italians whose methods he followed. But Inigo Jones stood by himself. His nephew and successor, John Webb, was a capable man and a fair draughtsman, but had little of the accomplishment and distinction of his master. Wren himself, though he became as he went on an excellent performer with T-square and compass, drew more as a skilful engineer than as an artist, and never showed any capacity as an imaginative draughtsman. In the All Souls and Soane collections are one or two good drawings of detail, probably by Grinling Gibbons ; but there is nothing to compare with the work of contemporary Frenchmen, nothing approaching the work of Jean Lepautre and Daniel Marot. Yet Wren himself drew much of his inspiration from the French, and there can be little doubt that in the second half of the seventeenth century, as in quite modern times, the French were the masters of the time in architectural draughtsmanship and set the standard of that art and established its finest tradition in every civilised country. It was France, too, that was first in the field, since the earlier days of the Renaissance, with those finely drawn and engraved examples of architectural details from the antique, such as Roland Fréart's famous *Parallel of Architecture* issued in 1651, or the admirable measured drawings of the *Édifices Antiques de Rome*

Chambord.   By Perelle

Vene du Chateau de Vaux le Vicomte du côte de l'Entrée.

A Paris chez I. Marette, Rue S. Jacque a la Victoire et chez lance Mariette.   Cum privilege du Roy.

View of Vaux le Vicomte.   By Perelle

made by Antoine Desgodetz, which appeared in 1682. Here (facing
p. 54) is an elevation and plan of a capital by Desgodetz, and it
is of interest to note that this young architect was sent out to
Rome by Colbert in 1675 at the King's expense to make measured
drawings of the remains of Roman architecture, and his book,
which is of considerable value to this date, is perhaps the first
and by no means the least valuable in the long list of brilliant
works produced by the students of the French Academy at
Rome. Incidentally, I may mention that Desgodetz, on his way
to Rome, was taken by the Turks and kept a prisoner at
Algiers for sixteen months. But the arm of the King was
long. Desgodetz was released and finally got to Rome and
made his drawings, which were engraved, on his return, at the
King's expense. The first twenty-five years of the reign of
Louis XIV. were a period of activity and high attainment in
all the arts such as had never been witnessed before in France,
and for which indeed the labours of French artists since the
end of the fifteenth century had been one long preparation.
It is a period that deserves the careful and intimate study of
all artists.

In the eighteenth century we shall find in Italy a draughtsman
of architecture of transcendent genius ; and towards the end
of the century Englishmen who could draw architecture better
than anyone in France or anywhere else at the time ; but
the work of the great French draughtsmen of the seventeenth
century has been too much neglected. Its historical importance
I have attempted to indicate in this chapter ; but its value and
suggestiveness to the architectural draughtsman are only to be
learnt by the study of their innumerable engravings. The
tendency among students to fly to the latest fashion in design
and drawing needs very careful watching, and it might be wise
for their teachers to urge them to turn their back for a time

on the present and the immediate past, and to extend their intellectual and imaginative horizon by studying the work of these half-forgotten artists. This might at least check one of the most crying faults in the practice of modern architecture —its ignorance of antiquity, its failure in the wider scholarship of art.

Chapiteau des Pilastres, dessiné sur l'angle

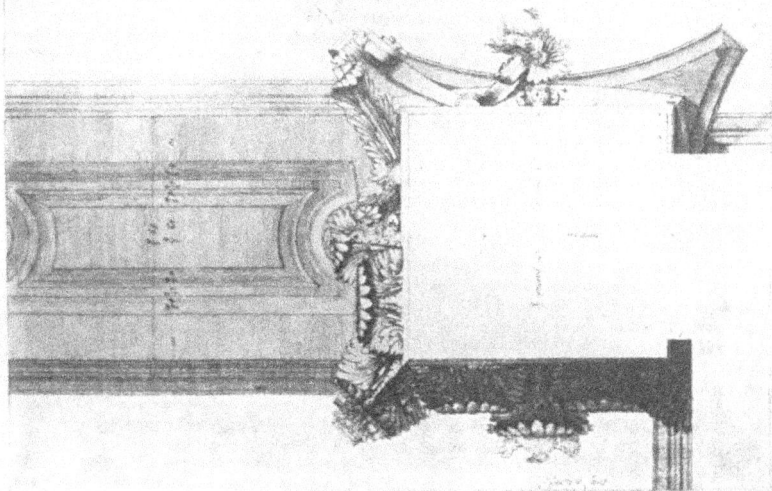

Plan du Chapiteau des pilastres vue par le dessus de l'architrave

From *Les Édifices Antiques de Rome.* By Antoine Desgodetz (Paris, 1682)

The Frontispiece of *Della Trasportazione dell' Obelisco Vaticano.* By Domenico Fontana (1589).

CHAPTER IV

ONE man dominates architectural draughtsmanship in the eighteenth century. In that century there were clever artists spinning out ornament in France, such as Meissonier and Oppenord, the Cuviliés, Huquier and La Londe, methodical and laborious architects such as Gibbs and Campbell issuing their ponderous volumes of solid architecture in England. There had been able draughtsmen in Italy, but above all towers the tremendous figure of Gian Battista Piranesi.

It is always tempting to think of the man of genius as arriving out of space, as a new force of unknown origin ; and Piranesi, more than almost any man, stands apart from his predecessors and contemporaries. There is about him something mysterious and dæmonic, yet he too comes under the law of history, and the temptation to detach him has to be resisted. However transcendent his achievements, whatever degree of perfection such a man may ultimately reach, careful study will show that he is the child of his age, and that his genius is revealed not least in the advance that he makes along a path already trodden by his predecessors. It is necessary, therefore, to retrace our steps, and pick up again the threads of Italian draughtsmanship at the end of the sixteenth century.

Within twenty years of the publication of Palladio's *Architettura*, in the year 1589, Domenico Fontana, the well-known architect of Sixtus V., brought out a folio of illustrations of the

55

means by which he had moved and set up the great obelisk of the Vatican, generally known as "the Guglia," in the Piazza of St. Pietro. The book opens with a splendid title page. In the centre is a portrait of Fontana, holding the obelisk ; on either side are composite columns on pedestals, supporting an entablature and a broken pediment, in the centre of which is a cartouche with the arms of the Pope, flanked by cheerful angels, gallantly straddling across the sides of the pediment. It is evident that we have before us the work of a draughtsman and engraver of a higher order than those who had worked for Serlio and Palladio, and this impression is confirmed by the remarkable drawings of the obelisk in the process of being raised, with its intricate shoring, its ropes, and its crowds of figures diligently working at the capstans. Fontana was perhaps the first to feel that fascination of scaffolding on which a well-known modern artist has played so skilfully. In our frontispiece is the obelisk, half-way up. Another plate shows it standing erect in all its glory, and finally Fontana gives a great folding plate, engraved by Natale Bonifacio of Siena, a sort of apotheosis of obelisks and columns in general, and more particularly of the noble efforts of Pope Sixtus V. This book of Fontana set up a new standard of architectural presentation, a method far ahead of the summary though suggestive wood-cuts of Palladio.

In the Soane collection there are three volumes containing the drawings made by Giovanni Battista Montano for his *Architettura*. Montano died at Rome in 1621 at the age of eighty-seven, and his book was published after his death in 1638, with a later edition in 1684. His drawings are free and capable, and deserve the attention of the student, but the exaggerations and mannerisms of seventeenth century Italian draughtsmanship already appear in his work.

The next stage was to abandon the formal method of Fontana's plates, and to introduce sky and landscape in combination with

FONTANA IN PIAZZA NAVONA.
Architettura del Cau. Gio. Lorenzo Bernini.

Fountain in the Piazza Navona. Rome. By G. B. Falda (b. 1648)

Cav. Gio. Lorenzo Bernini.

Drawing of a Fountain. Attributed to Lorenzo Bernini. In the Laing
Bequest, National Gallery of Scotland

architecture, a freer perspective, and more suggestion of the atmosphere and of light and shade. There are plates in Giovanni Battista Falda's *Fontane di Roma* in which the architecture is in correct perspective, and his figures and landscape excellent. In the plate of the fountain in the Piazza Navona he has attempted, not very successfully, some cumulus clouds ; but in this drawing the skilful arrangement of the light and shade is a genuine advance in architectural draughtsmanship. This plate, however, shows Falda at his best, for he was an unequal artist, and his tendency was to drop to a monotonous technique and to merely arbitrary conventions for his trees and skies. His work, as a rule, was inferior to that of the Perelle, but was very much better than that of his contemporaries in Italy. Falda was born in 1648, and was working at Rome between 1669 and 1691. In 1684 J. J. de Rubeis published in Rome a folio volume on the churches of Rome designed by M. Angelo, Bernini, Borromini, Pietro Berrettini, Rainaldi, and others, giving plans, sections, and elevations engraved by G. F. Venturini. The work was carelessly done and coarsely engraved. Architecture in Italy in the second half of the seventeenth century was becoming rather demoralised. To Fontana had succeeded Carlo Maderno, Bernini, Borromini, and Rainaldi, clever men enough in their exuberant and unscrupulous way, but not great architects or draughtsmen. Bernini, in spite of a period of failure and unpopularity, was far the most considerable figure among the artists of the two middle quarters of the seventeenth century. His word was law in France as well as in Italy, until the revolt of the French architects over the additions to the Louvre ; and probably no artist has ever obtained a position of such unquestioned supremacy. But Bernini was from the first a sculptor, and a sculptor who, almost by instinct, rebelled against restraint ; and though he did a great deal of architecture, some of it in a way of first-rate importance,

I

he never looked at things from the standpoint of an architect, and was one of the most conspicuous offenders among that not inconsiderable class of artists who have regarded architecture only as so much stage scenery. He felt his way to vaguely realised effects, and this failure, both in his training and in his habit of mind, is apparent in such of his architectural drawings as I have come across. The passion for dramatic effect, always latent in the Italian, began to assert itself in the seventeenth century with ever-increasing insistency, until it finally overpowered their sense of architecture, and substituted stage effects and the presentation of architecture for the Art itself. There were still able architects, such as Pietro Berrettini da Cortona (died 1669) who produced the fine design in the Uffizi for the transformation of the façade of the Pitti Palace, Longhena (died 1682) the architect of the Salute and the Palazzo Pesaro at Venice, or Bartolommeo Bianco (died 1656) the architect of the Palazzo del Universita at Genoa. But Italian architecture was on the wane. It had lost its serious purpose, and the slipshod architectural drawings of Bernini and Borromini are evidence of its failure. Borromini died in 1667, Bernini in 1680, the elder Rainaldi in 1655, the younger in 1691.

I do not wish to dwell unduly on the value of draughtsmanship, but I am convinced that unless a man is a competent draughtsman it is difficult for him to be a fine architect. I do not mean by this that an architect is to devote himself to turning out magnificent drawings; far from it, he has greater work to do. Rather, by a severe gymnastic of drawing, he should have trained his eye to the subtleties of form and composition, and his hand to interpret his ideas without hesitation and failure. Great painters do not parade their draughtsmanship, but it is implicit in their work. So, too, is it with architects; their draughtsmanship is shown in its highest form not merely in the beauty of their profiles, but in the scale, proportion, and composition of their buildings.

Drawing in pen and ink, perhaps by Perino del Vaga (Buonaccorsi, 1500-1547). In the Laing Bequest, National Gallery of Scotland

Drawing in pen and ink. Attributed to Perino del Vaga. In the Laing Bequest, National Gallery of Scotland

Pen and wash drawing of Altar-piece. By Teodoro Filippo da
Liagno (*b.* Madrid, 1556; *d.* 1625). In the Laing Bequest, National
Gallery of Scotland

But these qualities are only to be reached and fully realised through the assiduous study of great examples of the past, by means of which the architect accumulates a wealth of realised ideas in the background of his own imagination, trains his eye to seize at a glance the essential qualities of design, and his hand to interpret his conception, without those mischances and blunders which lie in wait for the incompetent draughtsman. Even if the latter is able to avoid these pitfalls by his knowledge, he is checked by his halting technique in the transmission of his ideas to those who have to carry them out. The purely technical architectural drawings (i.e. working drawings) made by such men as Bernini and Borromini are inferior to the drawings of Bramante, Peruzzi, and the two San Gallo. Those that I have seen are not worth reproducing, and it is evident that their authors were not real masters at any rate of this branch of their art, but were fumbling about for a motive in the hope of coming on it unawares in the tangle and confusion of their tentative lines. On the other hand, their dexterity in putting in figures and details of rococo ornament was amazing. Here is a sketch for a fountain attributed to Bernini, and another for a cartouche, possibly by Perino del Vaga, done straight off the reel, as it were, with a few strokes of the pen and a dexterous wash. This last drawing is not strictly an architectural drawing, but a brilliant sketch of a composition of figures to fill a given space; but it illustrates a quality of draughtsmanship which architectural students should aim at acquiring by drawing from the life in addition to technical architectural drawing. The same adroitness, carried further, appears in the altar piece by the Spaniard T. F. da Liagno, with its rather metallic treatment of the figures, and in the fine free drawing of the monument to Leo XI., by Algardi, the sculptor.

There can be little doubt, however, that towards the end of the seventeenth century the Italians had lost ground. The French, who earlier had followed them almost slavishly, had gone far beyond them, and there was nobody in Italy to rival the great French draughtsmen of the reign of Louis XIV. Indeed, in 1676 a Frenchman, writing from the French school at Rome, said there was scarcely an architect or a painter worth considering in Italy.

In the early part of the eighteenth century a good deal of lost ground was recovered, more particularly at Venice, or rather a new line was struck out in the topographical work of Antonio Canaletto and his school, and in the theatrical designs of the Bibiena family. Canaletto brought out a volume of etchings in 1741, containing ruins in the neighbourhood of Venice, and imaginary compositions. That Canaletto was an accomplished architectural draughtsman is, of course, well known, and his excellent method of drawing in line and wash is shown in the example which I reproduce from the British Museum collection, but as an etcher and engraver he was less successful. His method was conventional and dealt largely in crinkled lines laid side by side for skies, though sometimes, as in the "Torre del Malghera," he hit upon a very happy arrangement of light and shade. There was, however, little here to inspire his fellow-countryman, and there was still less in the dull and lifeless set of views of Venice, *Urbis Venetiarum prospectus celeberiores*, engraved by Venturini after Canaletto. Piranesi must have known of their existence, but from the very first, and even in his more formal engravings, he went far ahead of this tame and rather mechanical art. On the other hand, Piranesi had among his contemporaries several exceedingly capable draughtsmen of architecture, men who possessed a freedom and sureness of line scarcely inferior to that of their predecessors in the sixteenth century. Panini, for example, to whom I shall refer later, Mauro Tesi, and the Bibiena. Mauro Tesi was born near Modena in 1730, and died in 1766. The two drawings which I reproduce from the collection of the Royal

Design for Monument to Leo XI. By Algardi. In the Laing Bequest, National Gallery of Scotland

The Piazza of St. Mark's, Venice. By A. Canale, or Canaletto. British Museum

Drawing of Interior. By Mauro Tesi

Drawing of Court. By Mauro Tesi. In the Collection of the Royal Institute of British Architects

Drawing attributed to Vasari.   From a Volume of Drawings in the Soane Museum

Drawing of a Cartouche with figures (Italian, early Seventeenth Century).
In the Collection of the Royal Institute of British Architects

Institute of British Architects are as good as the sketches of Piranesi himself, and certain of the plates of the *Architettura* of Giuseppe Galli da Bibiena anticipated, to some extent, Piranesi's great architectural perspectives.

The Bibiena were a family of theatrical designers. The founder of the family, Giovanni Maria Galli, was born at Bologna in 1625, and died in 1665. He studied under Albani, and there are three drawings in the Uffizi attributed to him, of which, however, two are probably by his more famous grandson. Ferdinando Bibiena, probably the son of Giovanni, was born at Bologna in 1657, where he died in 1743. He studied under Cignani, and according to Bryan was employed by the Dukes of Parma and Milan and by the Emperor Charles VI. at Vienna ; but I incline to think that Bryan has mixed him up with Giuseppe Galli, who was undoubtedly chief theatrical engineer and architect to that Emperor at Vienna, and was much the ablest and most distinguished member of the family. The Royal Institute of British Architects is fortunate in possessing some thirty-one original drawings by this artist, in pen and wash, most of which show an astonishing ability in draughtsmanship and mastery of perspective. In 1740 he issued his folio of catafalques and theatrical scenery. The catafalques were enormous monuments under baldachinos, designed and beautifully drawn in line and wash by Bibiena, rococo in character, clearly and accurately engraved in plan, section, and elevation. Interspersed with these are fancy views of Roman Fora and theatrical scenes, which remind one of Inigo Jones's designs for masques, though far more elaborate—and perspectives of interiors and of staircases leading interminably upwards past tiers of galleries and under arcaded colonnades. It is probable that the palaces designed by Alessi and Bartolommeo Bianco, at Genoa, suggested these vistas to Bibiena. Daniel Marot had attempted something of the sort in his plates of the Palace of Apollo, of Mars, and of Perseus ; but it is more likely that his scenes were suggested by Italian designs than that they inspired Bibiena, whose drawings are of astounding intricacy and touched by that passion for great scale which was peculiar to the Italians. I give a fine example from the British Museum collection.

Bibiena developed his ideas in the true theatrical manner, and with amazing skill in perspective ; but his designs are much alike, and these limited motives appear to have exhausted his imagination. He was an artist of rather narrow range and of commonplace instincts apart from his sense of perspective, and his archæology was simply absurd. Probably it was not intended for anything else but stage scenery or those fancy compositions of architecture and landscape which had a considerable vogue with decorators in the early part of the eighteenth century, both in France and Italy. Piranesi, who was twenty-one when Bibiena's book was issued, must have been familiar with his work, and, I think, a good deal influenced by it in his early engravings. There is a drawing attributed to Piranesi in the British Museum which, if it was made by him, must have been a study from one of the plates in Bibiena's folio ; and Bibiena's mastery of intricate perspective, and skill in drawing the contortions of the most violent baroque, must have appealed to Piranesi as a draughtsman, however much he may have despised his designs as architecture. This architectural scenery for the stage, and the habit of painted architectural backgrounds and perspectives in decoration may have suggested to Piranesi some of his own compositions. On the other hand, their unreality, their failure in the sense of structure, must have repelled him, and there can be little doubt that their architectural inadequacy stimulated his fighting instincts to show, once and for all, how such things ought to be done.

Giovanni Battista Piranesi was born at Venice in 1720. His

A Theatrical Scene.   By Giuseppe Galli da Bibiena.   In the British Museum

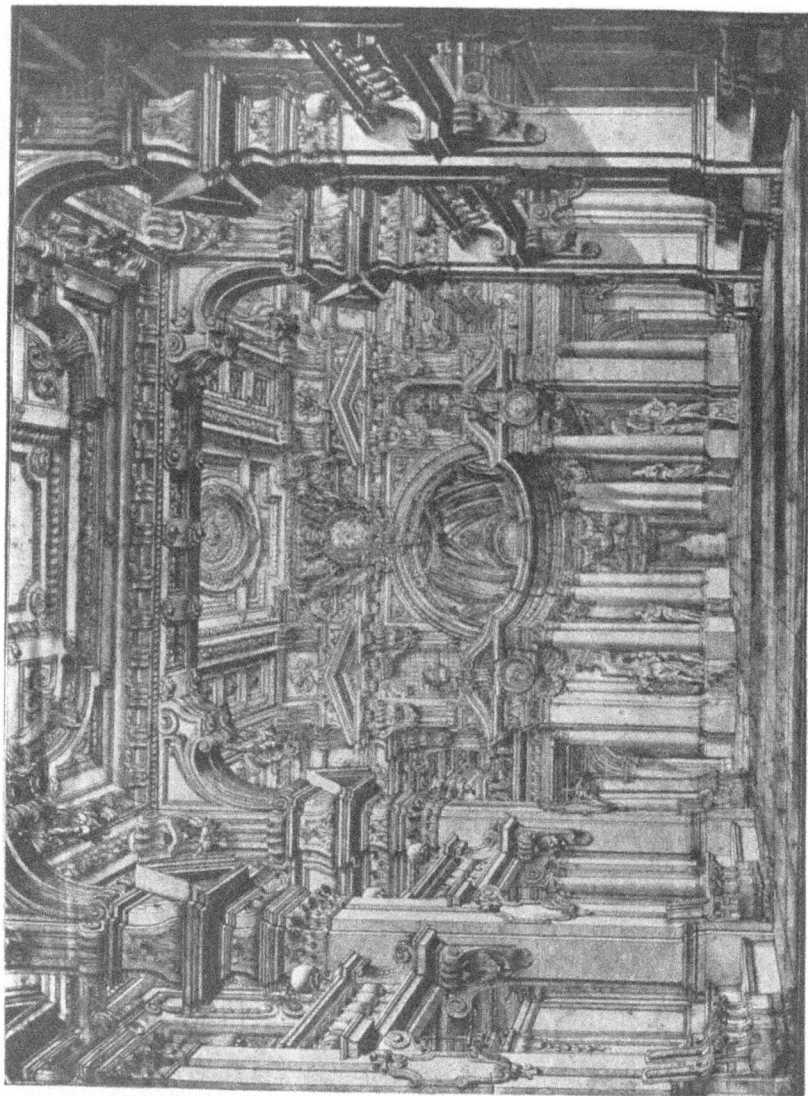

Drawing for Stage Scenery. By Giuseppe Galli da Bibiena. In the Collection of the Royal Institute

Drawing of a Catafalque. By Giuseppe Galli da Bibiena. In the Collection
of the Royal Institute of British Architects

Drawing for the angles of a Ceiling, probably by Giuseppe Galli da
Bibiena. In the Collection of the Royal Institute of British
Architects

Sketch by Giuseppe Galli da Bibiena. In the Collection of the Royal Institute
of British Architects

Drawing for Scenery. By Giuseppe Galli da Bibiena. In the Collection of the Royal Institute of British Architects

father was a mason, his mother the sister of the architect Lucchesi, under whom Piranesi is said to have worked for a time at Venice. His attention was thus directed to architecture from his earliest years, but he quarrelled with his uncle, and, being of a restless and ambitious nature, left Venice for Rome in 1738, and placed himself under a certain Valeriani, pupil of Sebastian Ricci, and an excellent master of perspective.* At this time Panini, who died in 1764, was at the height of his reputation, turning out compositions of ruins and figures, of no very great merit, but a good deal sought after for a certain respectable solidity and their harmless, if insipid, romance. He appears from his studies to have been an excellent draughtsman, and there is in the Panshanger collection an important picture of the interior of St. Peter's at Rome which shows that he was a past-master in perspective, and uncommonly dexterous with his figures. There are some good drawings by him in the Royal Institute of British Architects collection, one of which I reproduce and one which is in the Scottish National Gallery.† As in the case of Bibiena, Piranesi, who was the last man in the world to copy anyone, took up the theme of Panini and made it his own, and it was from the Ricci and Panini that Piranesi derived his fondness for composition of ruins, that search for the romantic element in classical materials which is so characteristic of the eighteenth century, and which ended in the almost total overthrow of the classical tradition. All sorts of stories are told of the youth of Piranesi. He was hot-blooded,

* Mariette (Abecedario) says that Joseph and Dominique Valeriani, Romans, were pupils of Ricci, and were chiefly employed in theatrical decorations. They are not mentioned in Bryan. Sebastian Ricci died in 1734. His nephew Marco, who always worked with him and accompanied him to England, died at Venice in 1729.

† The elder Panini (Giovanni Paolo) was born at Piacenza in or about 1691, and died in 1764. His son Giuseppe was born about 1745, and died about 1812. The drawings in the Royal Institute of British Architects are by the elder Panini and are bound up in the same volume as the drawings of Bibiena, Mauro Tesi, Soufflot, Servandoni, Louis and others.

reckless, and suspicious—a man of impulse, spurred on by a morbid imagination, who spent his life in controversy and quarrel. He is said to have attempted to murder Vasi, his master in engraving, because he believed that Vasi was withholding from him the secrets of his art.* On the other hand, he engaged himself literally at sight to the girl who afterwards became his wife. He appears to have left Rome, perhaps after his quarrel with Vasi, and returned to Venice, where he was said to have worked for a short time under Tiepolo. But Piranesi was a draughtsman pure and simple, and not a painter. Moreover, archæology had already got him in its net, and he set off on his travels again, first to Naples, thence to Paestum, returning to Rome apparently soon after 1740. Here he spent the remainder of his life, quarrelling with antiquaries and noble lords, but incessantly working, and rearing for himself, by his skill as a draughtsman and engraver, that monument, "aere perennius," which had been the admitted ambition of his life. He died in 1778.

Piranesi's earliest plates were issued in 1741. The well-known plate of the "Tempio Antico," the interior of a huge circular building with a broad flight of steps running round an inner circular shrine, was engraved in 1743. But his first serious publication of Roman antiquities and triumphal arches did not appear till 1748, followed by the Carcere d' Invenzione in 1750 ; and in 1751 his collected works up to date were published by Bouchard in a vast folio entitled Le magnificenze di Roma le piu remarcabili—a miscellaneous collection carelessly arranged, but splendidly printed on thick paper, with noble margins, perhaps the finest publication of architectural drawings that has ever been produced.† The

---

* Giuseppe Vasi, who was born in 1710, was only ten years the senior of Piranesi, and in 1745 was appointed engraver to the Court of Naples. He died in Rome in 1782.

† A copy of this magnificent work in my possession—which was turned out of the Radcliffe Library at Oxford a few years back by eminent men of science—contains, among many other plates, a splendid set of the rare first state of the Carcere series.

Drawing by P. Panini. In the Collection of the Royal Institute of British Architects

Drawing in line and wash. By P. Panini. In the Laing Bequest, National Gallery of Scotland

Drawing of a Ceiling (Italian, late Seventeenth Century). In the
Collection of the Royal Institute of British Architects

Drawing of Ceiling (Eighteenth Century). School of Giacomo Serpotta. In the Laing Bequest, National Gallery of Scotland

Piazza di Monte Cavallo.   By G. B. Piranesi

The Piazza di S. Pietro.   By G. B. Piranesi

Antichita Romane, in four volumes, containing 216 plates, appeared in 1756, and was dedicated in the first instance to Lord Charlemont ; but Piranesi considered Lord Charlemont's attitude so ungenerous that he removed his name, and afterwards dedicated the work to Robert Adam. In 1761 Piranesi, who now described himself as " Fellow of the Society of Antiquaries of London," brought out his huge volume of *Della magnificenza ed architettura de Romane*, in which he gave at great length his views of the origin of Roman architecture, and used his extraordinary ability as an etcher to demonstrate his quite erroneous argument.   The *Diverse Maniere d' adornare i Cammini*, etc., appeared in 1769, and the *Vasi, candelabri*, etc., in 1778, the year of Piranesi's death.   There are, of course, many other engravings given in the bibliographies, but these are his principal works, and the plates which I illustrate from Bouchard's edition of 1750–51, and from the *Magnificenza ed architettura*, are typical of the different phases of the work of this great artist.

Piranesi's temperament was so complex and turbulent that he was a man of many manners, and the problem of disentangling these is made more difficult by the fact that for years after his death his son Francisco continued to issue his father's plates with modifications of his own, and plates of his own from his father's drawings, just sufficiently like to be confused with his father's work by careless observers. Piranesi's best work is contained in Bouchard's folio.   He did an abundance of work after that date, much of it very accomplished, but finish and elaboration took the place of the tense emotion that lies concealed beneath the surface of the wonderful plates that he made in the ten years before 1750.   His manner ranges from the formal treatment of the Piazza of St. Peter's to the wild licence of the *Grotesche*, but between these two extremes there are all sorts of variations.   Even in his most restrained manner he could do wonders in the way

J

of suggesting texture and reflected lights, as in the plate of the
"Fountain of Trevi," and that of the "Portico of Octavia." Nor
was his success merely technical. In nearly all his plates he succeeded in conveying an impression of that great scale, and of the
magnificence of the buildings of ancient Rome, which from first to
last were the predominant motives of his work, and became with him
almost an obsession. The figures of the "Monte Cavallo," poised
against the setting sun, show his power of imparting to all that
he did a certain epic quality, some feeling of an heroic age long
past that haunted his imagination, even to the tainting of its
sanity. For even in these engravings, severely conventional in
their method, the wild man is lurking, barely restrained by respect
for scholarship. In the foreground of the view of St. John Lateran
appear three ragged and villainous figures that Callot might have
drawn, and here they are again in the foreground of the Colosseum.
Elsewhere wild figs cover the ruins, thick tufts of weeds crown
the ruined apse of the Temple of Isis, and behind it is a great
white cloud, vibrant with the light of an Italian sky. In those
beautiful little etchings from the first and second parts of the
*Antichita Romane,** the Romanticist—or perhaps I should say the
purely imaginative artist—breaks loose, and gives full expression
to his joy in light and shade and movement, and to his sense of
the nobility of architecture shown high against the sky ; witness
the splendid treatment of the Arch of Titus, with the great label
in the left-hand corner, the stone pine by the tomb of Cecilia Metella,
the Arch of Trajan on the mole at Ancona, with the strange ship-
ping in the foreground. Even so, the fire within him was not
satisfied. Buildings and Nature herself seemed to check the swing
of his imagination. He seems for a time to have tired of all
restraint, and in the *Invenzioni Capric di Carceri*, the caprices

* These were suggested by the series of views of Rome and Venice made by
Israel Silvestre in the middle of the 17th century.

Veterum...qua...Marciae ductuum, muris Urbis, ab Aurelianó constructis
...nuae, á Porta Majori ad Portam S.Laurentii; prout habetur in Tom. I. An-
...tiqu.Rom.num.119,120,121 Indic. gener.verig.Romæ veteris.

The Aqueduct of Aurelian. By G. B. Piranesi. From the *Romanorum* **Magnificentia**

The Colosseum. By G. B. Piranesi

Title-page for the *Capric di Carceri*. Drawn by G. B. Piranesi

Plate II. in the *Capric dl Carceri.* By G. B. Piranesi

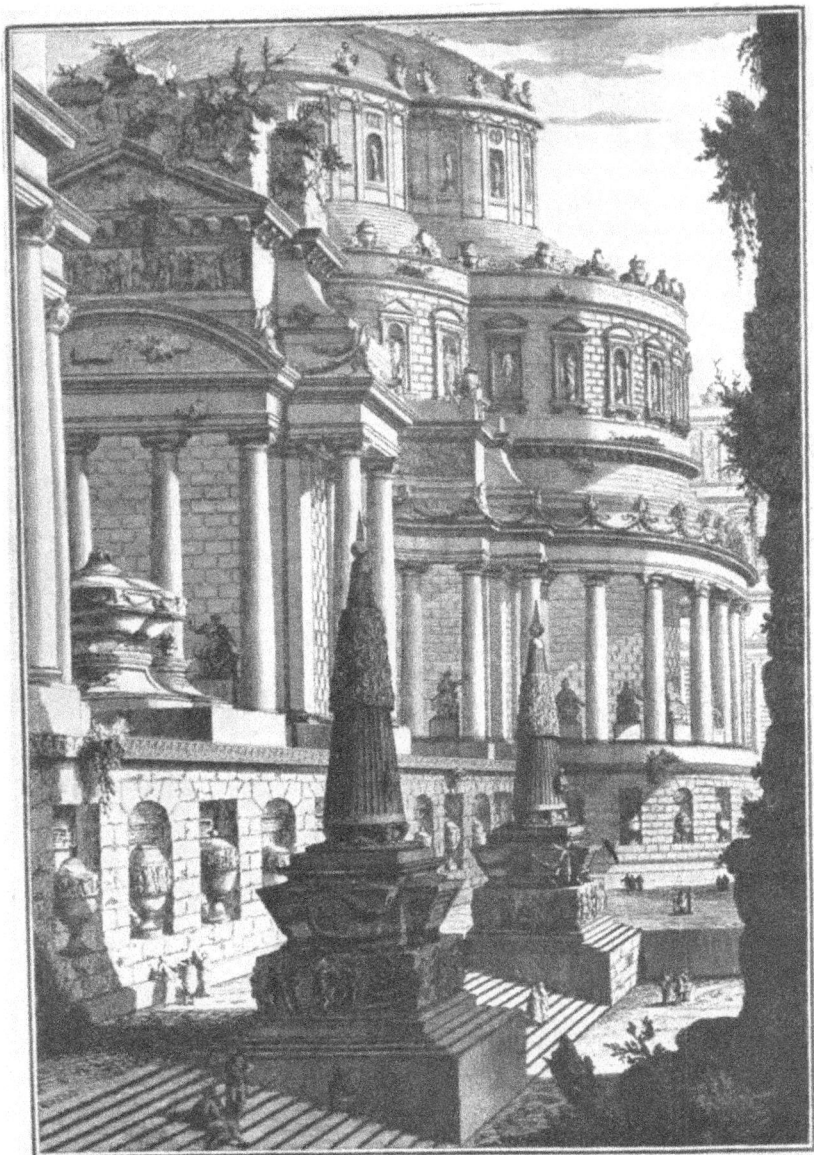

"Mausoleo Antico," as Engraved by G. B. Piranesi

"Mausoleo Antico," as Drawn by G. B. Piranesi (*not* Canaletto). In the
National Gallery of Scotland

and variations on a prison theme, he let himself go, in a world that never has been or could be—a world of terrifying nightmare, of huge incoherent and terrifying forms. His needle must have raced over the copper, searching but never grasping the vague immense idea that haunted his imagination. Perhaps Piranesi himself could not have told us the meaning of his first plate, the circular opening above with the figures impaled on the rim, and the dragon's head ; or of that other plate, with the tortured figures writhing on the broken arch, and the pulley of sinister purpose that appears again and again in the prison series. In Bouchard's folio, these are followed by one of the wildest and most horrible drawings ever made, the first of the *Grotesche*. A grinning skeleton lies in the foreground, another is dipping his hand into a moss-grown urn ; to the left, with his back turned to the spectator, a mighty Hercules is facing a satyr, a beam of light traverses the drawing from left to right, and high up on the right part of the belt of the Zodiac shows against a background of trees. It was a work dangerously near insanity, and Piranesi only allowed himself three more such plates ; but surely the etched line has never done more.

Nor has anyone ever approached Piranesi in his power of drawing architecture. He is said to have worked direct on the copper without preliminary sketches. This, however, is certainly not true of all his work. There is an exquisite drawing of his in the British Museum, in line and wash, a preliminary study for one of his smaller etchings ; and I discovered, in the Scottish National Gallery, his drawing for the plate of the " Mausoleum of a Roman Emperor," wrongly attributed to Canaletto. This drawing is a masterly sketch in line and wash, altered in certain details on the finished plate. I reproduce the original drawing, and the engraving made from it reversed in the print and with several variations in the upper part of the plate. In the same collection there is a study in pen and wash for the prison series, suggestive of the second plate, but never carried out in any one of them. It is a characteristic and astonishing drawing. Some of our our modern draughtsmen use the blot, but too often only as a cloak for ideas imperfectly realised. But in Piranesi's drawing they are the instantaneous transcript of some burning thought, each stroke of the pen and sweep of the brush tells its story ; it is the work of a man who thought in terms of architecture, whose imagination lived habitually in a world of vast spaces and giant forms.

Piranesi is an artist whose reputation, long ago established and for a time overlooked, has now more than recovered its place, but I think he has been sometimes admired for the wrong qualities. An enthusiastic claim has recently been made for him as the founder of modern classical architecture, as the inspirer not only of Robert Adam, but of neo-classic as handled by our colleagues in America. This is going large with a vengeance. It is true that Adam for a time came under the influence of Piranesi, and even attempted perspective drawings in his manner, of which examples are to be seen in the Soane Museum, which entirely fail to catch the spirit of their original. Adam was not the man for this sort of work. He was a careful and accomplished mechanical draughtsman, with a great deal of ability, but not in this direction. His temperament was as far removed from that of Piranesi as the North Pole from the South. The plates made by a certain Rossini early in the nineteenth century in imitation of Piranesi are the merest travesty of that unequalled master. As for recent American architecture, brilliant as it often is, it is based almost entirely on the teaching of the École des Beaux-Arts. The only direct follower of Piranesi was Sir John Soane, who, in the curiously heavy and lifeless orna- ment of the Bank of England, suggests the details of Roman architecture that Piranesi illustrated with such elaborate industry.

Piranesi was not, in fact, a practical designer at all. His imagination revelled in gigantic agglomerations of classical motives,

Tomb of Cæcilia Metella. By G. B. Piranesi. From the *Antichità Romane fuori di Roma*

The Arch of Titus. By G. B. Piranesi. From the *Antichità Romane di tempi della Repubblica* (1748)

From the *Grotesche*. By G. B. Piranesi

Ancona.   By G. B. Piranesi

piling up mountainous buildings that towered among the clouds ; but I doubt if, among all his inventions of buildings, there is a single one that would be of real use to an architect, and his combinations of details were licentious in the last degree. There is a pen-and-ink drawing in the British Museum which shows the uncertain quality of his taste. Two Doric columns, very ill-designed, support a disproportionate entablature without an architrave, which projects far outside the shaft of the columns—a bad mistake for any classicist to make ; and at the bottom, just above the base, the columns pass through a huge oblong stone carved on all four sides. The draughtsmanship is superb, the design about as bad as it is possible to imagine. Piranesi's direct influence on design—that is, the motives that he may have provided for immediate conversion into detail—I believe to have been almost entirely for the bad. It resulted in that dull and—if I may be excused the word—stodgy classic that prevailed in England in the early part of the last century, and appeared in quite another form in the pedantic and finicking designs of Percier and Fontaine. It is not here, nor in his laborious and misguided archæology, that Piranesi's greatness is to be found, or his interest as an artist.

In the frontispiece of one of the Temples with which he adorned his answer to Mariette (in a controversy, by the way, in which Piranesi was entirely wrong), he has placed in a cartouche a quotation from Le Roy, " *pour ne pas faire de cet art sublime un vil métier.*" Piranesi did not consider architecture as an organic art working under practical conditions, an art which derives its strength and interest from the fact that it has to realise certain well-defined ends ; but, on the other hand, no one ever possessed a keener sense of the dignity of architecture and of its poetry. The quality of genius, which raised him above other artists, was shown not only in his assured and astonishing technique, but in a certain imaginative outlook on architecture—in his conception of it as a great and even stupendous art, full of mystery, full of a profound beauty and poetry, that will only reveal itself to the initiated. It was not the *Magnificenze Romane*, but the *Carcere*, that inspired the younger Dance to design Newgate, those visions of a peculiar hell that for once stimulated a merely mechanical practitioner to scale heights inaccessible to all but men of genius. It is by his quality of fervent imagination that Piranesi retains his place of fame, when dexterous men such as Giuseppe Galli are almost forgotten ; and his interest will always be partly psychological. He was obsessed by the megalomania that has always held the Italians, and by their instinct for dramatic effect. To Piranesi, architecture presented itself less as building than as some tremendous stage effect, free from the fetters of practical conditions, huge, titanic, immeasurable, far remote from everyday life. But, apart from this, there is an element in his work quite personal and individual. What was it that drove him out to the savage ferocity of his conceptions ? Those squalid beggars lurking amid the ruins, those rocks that slowly shape themselves as portentous figures—ghastly suggestions of corruption and decay ?

In the portrait opposite to the title page of Bouchard's folio, Piranesi has the head of a prize-fighter, and there is a wild glare in his eye which suggests that insanity was here not far from the surface. Yet the facts are otherwise. Long after the *Grotesche* and the *Carcere*, Piranesi pursued his labours with a tenacity of purpose and restraint impossible to associate with madness. Though his work sometimes seems to totter on the brink of insanity, I do not think that the answer is here. Piranesi was a man of extraordinary gifts, and of a very complex nature. He would assuredly have reckoned himself a classicist of unimpeachable purity. Yet, in fact, he was steeped in unconscious romanticism. What else is the meaning of these weird figures, of his care for sky and clouds? When he drew Aurelian's Aqueduct as an illustration to a learned treatise, he could not resist the temptation to put two figures gesticulating in the foreground, and a stone pine as fine as any that Turner ever drew. The man knew himself imperfectly, and I believe that his most characteristic work was the result of this romantic strain—of a certain fury of temperament, impatient perhaps of the frippery and insincerity of life at Rome in the eighteenth century; and of a rather noble ambition, that led this artist, who knew every moulding and detail of antiquity in Italy, to turn his back on it all and feel his way to something grander than detail, to that unknown spirit which, to his fevered mind, seemed still to haunt the ruins of Roman greatness. Piranesi was a great artist, one of the greatest in his way, and all draughtsmen will study him for his amazing technique and his extraordinary powers of imagination. Yet there is no artist who should be approached with more care and discrimination. Those who have endeavoured to imitate him—his son, Rossini, and others—have failed disastrously. The bow of Ulysses is for Ulysses alone. The art of Piranesi is not a manner to be learnt: it was the intensely personal expressions of a wild and melancholy genius.

CHAPTER V

THE isolation of England is as apparent in the development of architectural drawing as it is in the history of other branches of the arts. As compared with the Continent, neo-classic architecture arrived late in this country. When Charles II. came to the throne, the arts were disorganised. Only John Webb was left to carry on the tradition of Inigo Jones. Wren was a brilliant young amateur, who had yet to learn his art ; and though he undoubtedly owed a great deal to the artists collected by Colbert for Louis XIV., English architecture followed its course unaffected in the main by the astonishing attainment of the arts in France. With the Revolution of 1688 the Dutch influence came in, and obtained a firm hold of English vernacular architecture ; but meanwhile a reaction was setting in against the free classic of Wren. The severest version of Palladianism became the fashion, and in the early part of the eighteenth century the object of every ambitious architect was to produce buildings in the strict classical manner, according to the teaching of Vitruvius, filtered through Palladio. With such ideals, they had no use for the luxuriant imagination and the splendid draughtsmanship of Marot and Lepautre. Exact and methodical geometrical drawings gave them all that they needed, with the result that the architectural draughtsman and designer such as Lepautre never had a chance in England ; and there arose a school of mechanical draughtsmen on the one hand, and on the other the topographical artist who gradually merged into the painter, pure and simple. Towards the end of

A Study for the *Carceri*. By G. B. Piranesi

A Proscenium.   By Inigo Jones (1634).   In the Collection of the Royal Institute
of British Architects

the eighteenth century, architectural draughtsmanship in England
recovered itself, and reached a degree of excellence perhaps higher
than that of any other country, but it did so by paths that were
curiously indirect, and which started from two different and even
opposite points of view.

The collection of drawings by Thorpe, now in the Soane
Museum, is the first collection of systematic architectural drawings to be found in this country. The drawings in this collection
are probably the work of several men, and are of considerable
archæological but small artistic interest. Nor is it material,
from the point of view of draughtsmanship, whether they represent designs by Thorpe, or whether, as I maintain, they are
surveys of existing buildings, made on somewhat similar lines to
Du Cerceau's drawings for his *Plus Excellents Bastimens*, though
altogether inferior in technique. The draughtsman has little to
learn from this collection,* and we may pass on to the drawings
of Inigo Jones, probably much the best English draughtsman of
the seventeenth century, and an artist more in advance of his time
than perhaps any in the history of English art, for the Banqueting
House was designed and built when the Jacobean manner was
still rampant in England. His faithful pupil and relation, John
Webb, says, " Mr. Jones was generally learned, eminent for architecture, a great geometrician, and in designing with his pen (as
Sir Anthony Van Dyck used to say) not to be equalled by whatever great masters in his time, for boldness, softness, sureness,
and sweetness of his touching." As a matter of fact, the figure
drawings in the Chatsworth sketch-book have some rather bad
mannerisms, an unpleasant line, cross-hatching, lumpy muscles,
and other faults which he probably picked up from contemporary
Italians ; but in certain of his drawings for proscenia, and in some

---

* The reader will find the results of my examination of these drawings stated
in Ch. III. Vol. I. of my *History of Renaissance Architecture in England.*

K

of his architectural projects, he shows a mastery of hand and a knowledge of what he was doing, which go far to justify Webb's praise, and his drawings may well have been a revelation to his contemporaries in England. He drew with extraordinary freedom and rapidity, whether it was details of architecture, or designs for the costumes and scenery of masques, and in nearly all his compositions for the latter there is a strong decorative sense and feeling for composition. Inigo Jones did for the Court of Charles I. what Berain was to do for that of Louis XIV., and Bibiena for the Court of Vienna. But the Englishman's work has more distinction and a finer sense of style than is found in that of either the Frenchman or the Italian. I give an example of his designs for scenery of masques designed for the Queen's *Masque of Indianos*, 1634. It is very freely sketched in ink and wash without any attempt at finish. In the Duke of Devonshire's collection at Chiswick there is a drawing* of stage scenery showing an open court with fountains, designed in a manner that anticipates, by nearly a hundred years, Bibiena's designs for the Court theatre at Vienna. It is an admirable and very remarkable drawing, such as no one in France at the time, and few men in Italy, could have designed and drawn; indeed, there are qualities in this design, and in the sketch for a ceiling at Wilton by Inigo Jones, ahead of anything done in France before François Mansart found himself at Blois.

Inigo Jones's architectural drawings are a difficult problem. There are few drawings actually signed by him, while there are a number of drawings in the Duke of Devonshire's collection, and at Worcester College, Oxford, of buildings which have always been attributed to Inigo Jones, but which are signed for all to see, "John Webb, Architect," and there is no doubt that these

* Reproduced with other drawings of Inigo Jones, in an article by me in *The Portfolio* in 1889.

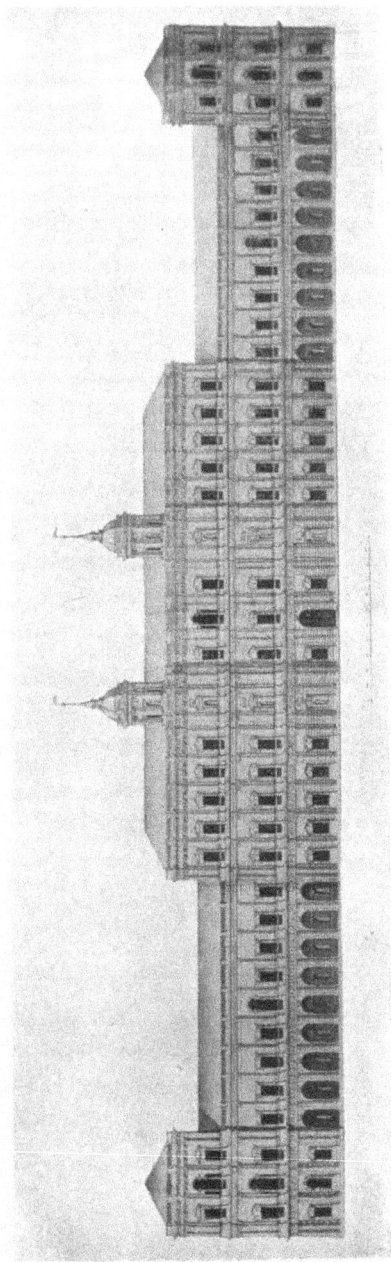

Drawing of Whitehall. By Inigo Jones. In the Worcester College Collection

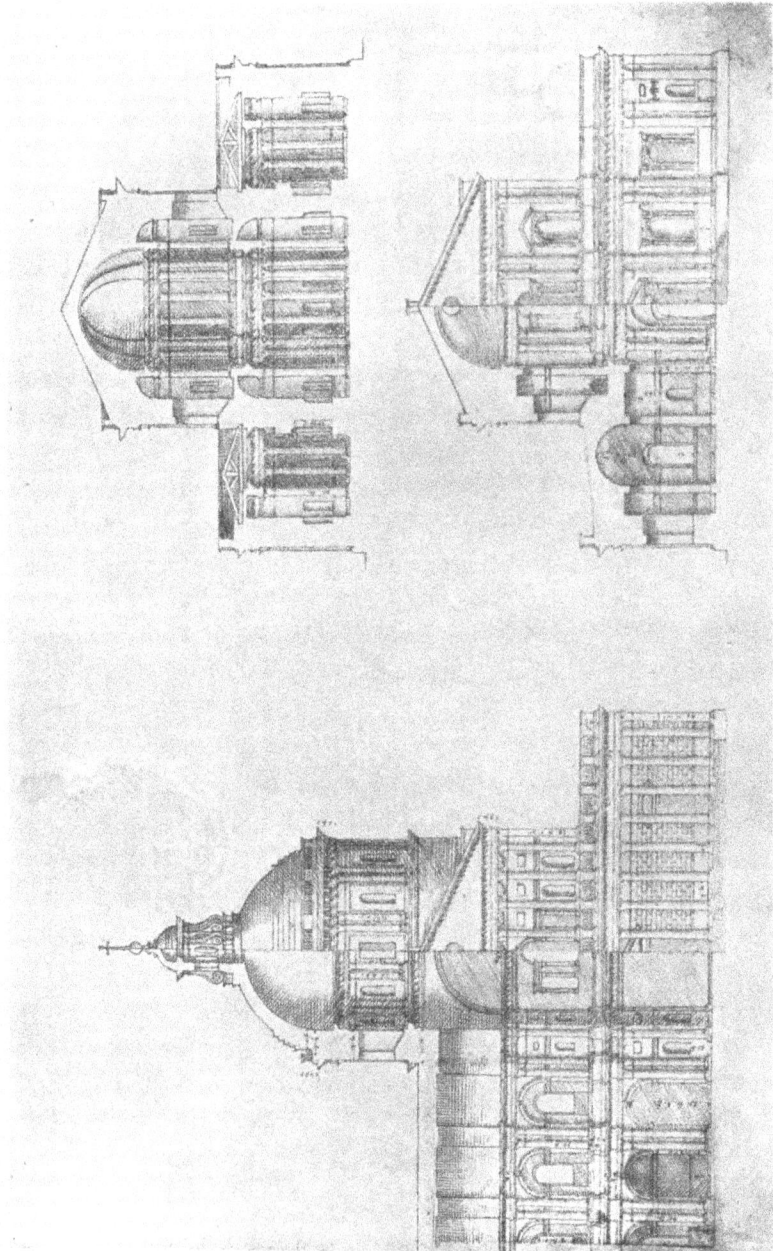

Studies for a Church. By Inigo Jones. In the Worcester College Collection

were made by Webb. On the strength of this, and of certain claims made by Webb when applying for the surveyorship after the Restoration, Mr. Gotch has gone so far as to raise the whole question of the Whitehall designs, apart from the Banqueting House. The reproductions issued by Kent and Campbell in the eighteenth century are, of course, not to be trusted. Historical accuracy was less their aim and ideal than the presentation of a set of plates agreeable to the taste of the *cognoscenti* of the time, and they had some excuse in the confusion that undoubtedly prevailed in the miscellaneous collection of drawings with which they had to deal. In the Worcester collection authentic drawings by Inigo Jones are mixed up with copies and variations by Webb, and studies for an amended scheme which Webb appears to have prepared at some time near the end of the Civil War. A careful study of the technique of these drawings convinces me that Inigo Jones did, in fact, make the designs for the Palace of Whitehall, and that the drawings 1—6 in the Worcester collection are his handiwork. Inigo Jones could draw the figure very well in the free manner he had learnt in Italy ; John Webb had little or no idea of it. Drawing No. 5 shows a section E and W through the courts behind the river front, including the circular court. In this example the caryatides are drawn in a masterly way beyond the draughtsmanship of Webb, who could not even draw them when he had the originals to copy. This drawing is clearly by the same hand as the other drawings, 1—6, and that hand was, I am convinced, the hand of the master, not of the pupil. Inigo Jones had two methods of architectural drawing. The first was with pen and line, based on the manner of Palladio and the younger San Gallo. This is shown in the drawing of a church on the plan of a Greek cross, No. 38, and in drawings Nos. 44 and 45. In more finished drawings he used a very fine line and a faint wash. Unfortunately, examples of this second method are so faded that it is impossible to reproduce them properly. The drawing No. 5 is a beautiful example, and the reproduction of the elevation of Whitehall from roll No. 12 gives some idea of this very delicate and accomplished draughtsmanship. John Webb's drawings, of which the best are his details of ceilings and chimney-pieces for Greenwich,* show that he was a fairly competent draughtsman, but that the figure was beyond him; and though he was a considerable architect, his inferiority in draughtsmanship was but a part of a general inferiority in imagination, and in artistic refinement and sensibility, to that great and very distinguished artist, Inigo Jones.

Wren, who by a discreditable intrigue was preferred to Webb for the post of Surveyor-General, was at the time of his appointment the merest amateur, both in architecture and draughtsmanship; and though in architecture he rose to unequalled eminence, he never was a fine draughtsman. A careful study of the drawings in the All Souls and Soane Museum collections leads me to think that he relied largely on such men as Grinling Gibbons for his detail.† The drawing in the All Souls collection of the design for St. Paul's, with the open pine-apple at the top, dated 1666, is by Wren himself, and is as bad in drawing as it is in design. The "Warrant" design, made in 1675, "*juxta tertiam propositionem,*" shows a considerable advance in both. Drawing No. 12 (Vol. II.), drawn with a fine line and wash, is a perfectly competent geometrical drawing, and may be taken as representing the standard of Wren's attainments as a draughtsman, beyond which I can find no evidence that he ever advanced. The fine drawing of the west front of St· Paul's,‡ which I reproduce, was probably not made by Wren.§ In

* In the Chiswick collection. These are dated 1663, 1666, and 1668.
† *See* Vol. I., Drawing 91, All Souls collection, and details in the Soane Museum.
‡ Vol. II., 39, All Souls collection.
§ The faint, but very skilful, perspective drawings of the interior of St. Paul's, in pencil, are probably studies by a later hand for an engraving. The difficulty with these

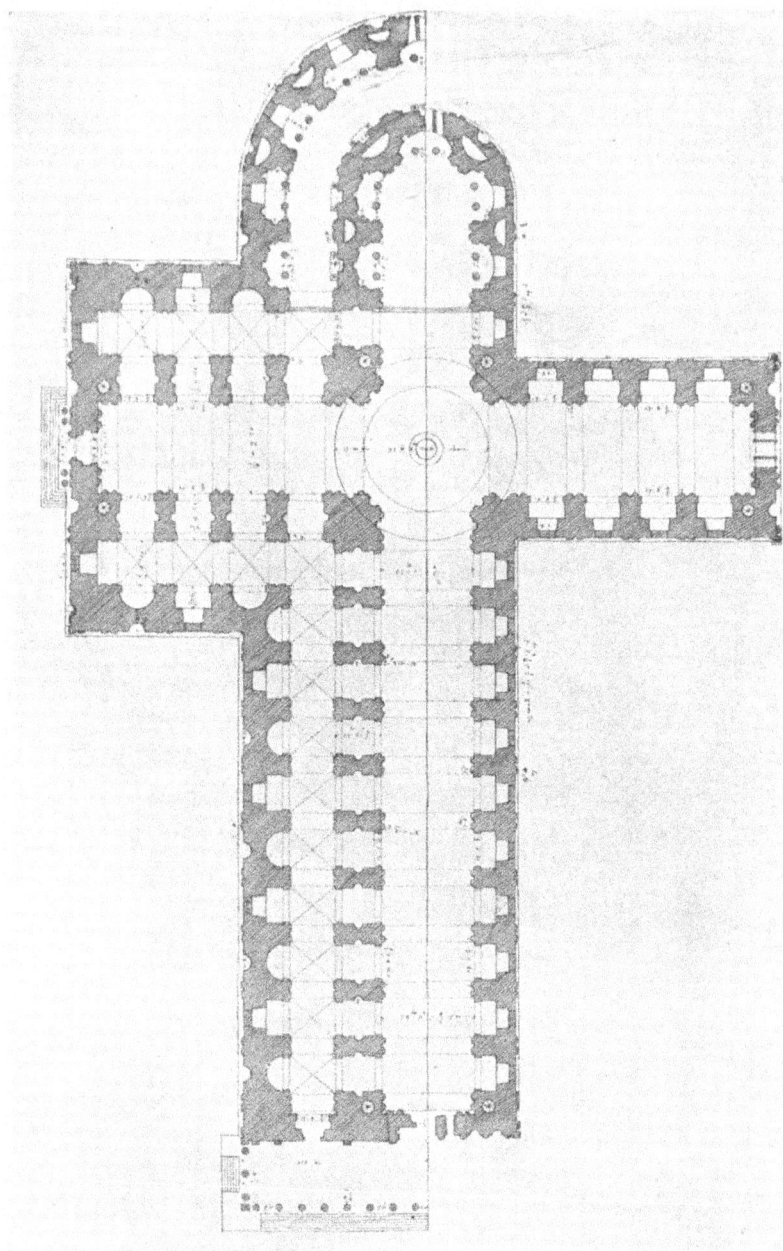

A Plan by Inigo Jones. In the Worcester College Collection

"Warrant" Design for St. Paul's Cathedral. By Wren.
At All Souls' College, Oxford

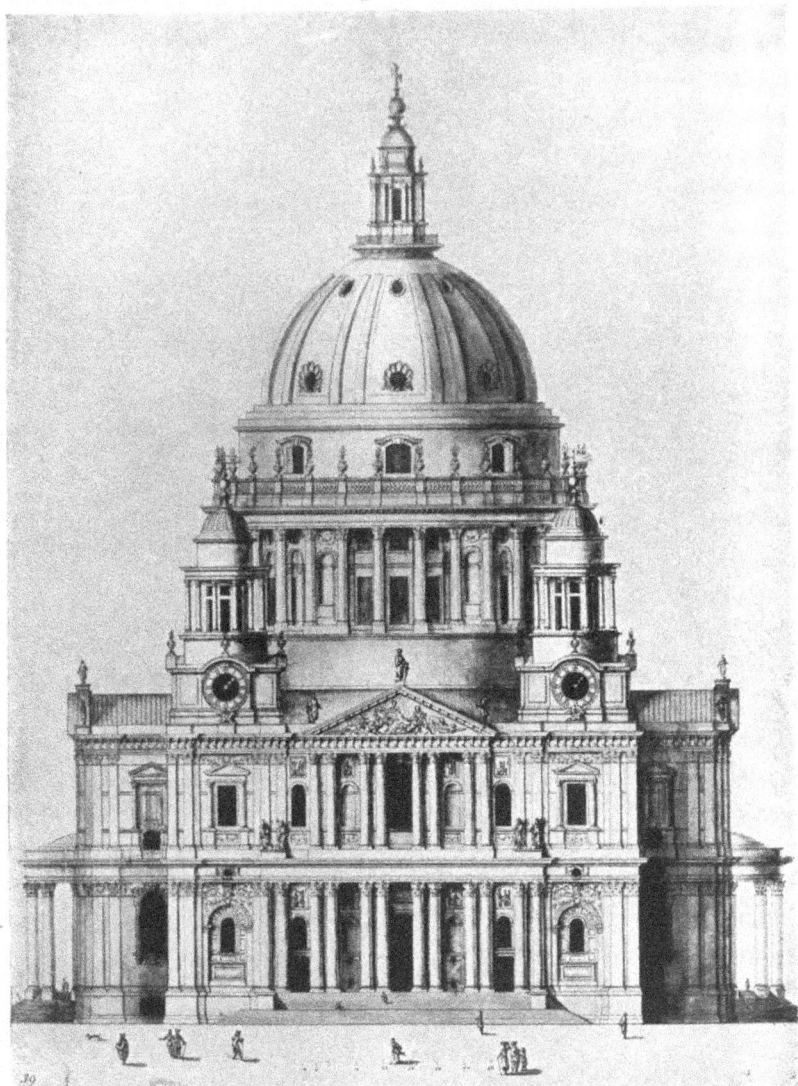

A Drawing of the West Elevation of St. Paul's Cathedral.   Contemporary
with Wren.   At All Souls' College, Oxford

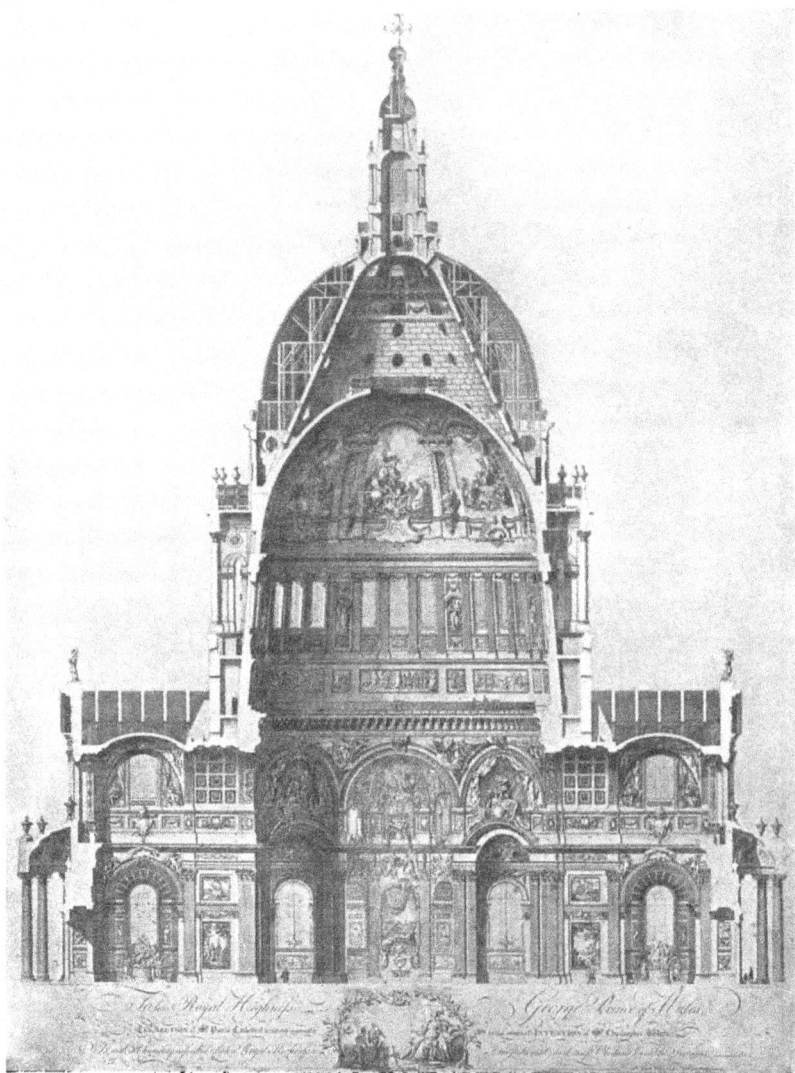

Section of St. Paul's Cathedral. Drawn by S. Wale, and the decoration by
J. Gwynn (1755). Engraved by E. Rooker

spite of the profound admiration that I feel for Wren's astonishing genius, I cannot help thinking that the lack of finish and scholarship occasionally to be noted in his architectural detail was due to his very moderate capacity as a draughtsman. His technique was inferior to his intellect. Had he added to his attainments the sweep of line and the trained and delicate artistic sense of Inigo Jones, his achievements would surely have been greater than those of any architect since the days of Imperial Rome.

It does not appear that there was anyone in England in the seventeenth century capable of taking up architectural draughtsmanship at the point where Jones had left it. Webb, who caught a faint reflection of his manner, was the only Englishman who attained even moderate accomplishment, according to modern standards of criticism, and the result of this, and of a growing academical tendency which culminated in the pedantry of the Burlington clique, was that architectural draughtsmanship in England split up into two camps. The architects devoted themselves to geometrical drawings, while a new school of topographical draughtsmen came into existence from which there ultimately emerged, in the latter part of the eighteenth century, the great English school of water-colour painting.

The series of large folio volumes of plates, with brief introductory letterpress, began, early in the eighteenth century, with Colin Campbell's famous *Vitruvius Britannicus*. The first two volumes were published in 1717, the third in 1725. They contained two hundred plates, " engraved by the best hands, and drawn either from the buildings themselves, or from the original

miscellaneous collections of drawings, mostly unsigned, and of varying degrees of excellence, is to disentangle the authentic work. The only solution is to use the technique of the undoubted drawings as a touchstone for the rest. There are a few signed drawings by Wren in the All Souls and Soane Museum collections, and my criticism is based on a study of the draughtsmanship shown in these examples.

designs of the architects."*   Colin Campbell made the drawings,
the majority of which were engraved by H. Hulsbergh, and the
result, within its limits, was a very fine work, splendidly printed,
and invaluable for the student of English architecture. The geometrical drawings, plans, and elevations are perfect in their way,
the detail drawn with full knowledge, and the tone of the shading
carefully regulated to avoid any falsification of the façade as a
whole. Geometrical drawings have sometimes been made in which
the shadows are greatly exaggerated and the window-openings
shown black, with the result that the design loses its breadth.
These faults are apparent in some of the elevations of Woolfe
and Gandon's continuation, forming Vols. IV. and V. (1767) of
the *Vitruvius Britannicus,* and in the later publications of the
eighteenth century. Campbell was too well trained in the classic
of his time, and was too intelligent an architect, to make any such
mistake. The "General Front of Blenheim," Greenwich Hospital, and Castle Howard † are beautiful drawings in their way,
and are not inferior to equivalent illustrations in Blondell's *Maisons
de Plaisance* (1737), published twenty years later. Campbell as
a perspective draughtsman was quite another thing. He had no
sense of atmosphere, movement, or light and shade ; and as soon
as he gave up his compass and T-square he was lost. The only
merit of his perspectives is the precision of their drawing of architecture. "The Prospect of the Royal Hospital at Greenwich" is
the best of them, but it is an extremely mechanical performance.‡
  Meanwhile, James Gibbs, who had been ignored by his brother
Scot, was at work on a volume of his own designs, which appeared
in 1728, with the title of *A Book of Architecture,* "undertaken,"
Gibbs informs us, "at the instance of several persons of quality
and others." Gibbs made the drawings ; Harris, Kirkall, Hulsbergh, and others engraved them ; and there is little to choose in

* Title pages, Vols. I. and II.   † Vol. I., Plates 58, 68, and 83.   ‡ Vol. III., Plate 2.

The Prospect of the Royal Hospital at Greenwich. By Colin Campbell. From *Vitruvius Britannicus* (Vol. I.)

The General Front of Blenheim. By Colin Campbell. From *Vitruvius Britannicus* (Vol. I.)

A Perspective View of St Martins Church.

St. Martin's in the Fields.   By James Gibbs.   From Gibbs's *Book of Architecture*

technique between the plates of Gibbs's book and those of Colin Campbell's, except that Gibbs was more successful in his perspectives, as in the excellent straightforward view of St. Martin's Church.* How much these architects owed to their engravers it is impossible to say in the absence of the original drawings; but I venture to think, from the family resemblance of the plates in most of the great eighteenth century architectural folios, they owed a good deal. Hulsbergh worked for Campbell and for Gibbs; Fourdrinier† for Castell, whose *Villas of the Ancients* appeared in the same year as Gibbs's *Book of Architecture* (1728), and for Kent, whose volume of designs by Inigo Jones appeared the year before, and included plates by Hulsbergh from drawings by Flitcroft.

The connoisseurs of the eighteenth century ran their men much as a racing man would run his horses, but a genuine interest in architecture must have existed to make these very costly publications possible. They continued to appear at intervals throughout the eighteenth century. Isaac Ware issued various plates of buildings, and further designs by Inigo Jones. In 1756 he issued his *Complete Body of Architecture*, and two years later Chambers published his *Treatise on Civil Architecture*. James Paine's two great folios of buildings erected from his designs appeared in 1767, and in 1778 appeared *The Works in Architecture of Robert and James Adam*, the last and most important effort at advertisement that appeared in the eighteenth century. Robert Adam was a dexterous draughtsman, and the student will find innumerable examples of his work in the Soane Museum. His drawings have the merit of extreme care and trained knowledge, and have their value for the student as a corrective against slipshod and slovenly workmanship. They are not, however, particularly stimulating, nor are they suggestive. Nothing is left to the imagination; everything is

* *Book of Architecture*, plate 1.
† Fourdrinier also engraved the plates of Gibbs's *Bibliotheca Radcliviana*, 1747.

finished with laborious completeness, and the effect is depressing and even paralysing. Drawings for engravers in the eighteenth century were usually made in line and wash; and the engravers were usually better men than the draughtsmen. The section of Kedleston, from *Vitruvius Britannicus*, Vol. IV., is typical of this work—exact and excellent so far as it goes, but of no very great value to the architectural draughtsman as distinct from the designer, because its merit is technical, and it is impossible to disentangle the value of the original drawing.*

The same criticism applies to those remarkable works—remarkable, that is, in regard to the time when they were undertaken—Wood and Dawkin's *Palmyra* (1755) and *Baalbec* (1757), Adam's *Spalatro*, Stuart and Revett's *Athenian Antiquities*, and Revett's *Antiquities of Ionia*. At a time when the attention of Continental artists and scholars was concentrated on Italy—that is, on Rome—with rare digressions to Magna Græcia, these Englishmen and Scotsmen had the courage and originality to go farther afield, and to lay the foundation of researches in the history of architecture which are still very far from completion. For the draughtsman, however, their value is small. The Royal Institute of British Architects possesses the original drawings from which the plates in the works of Wood and Dawkin and Stuart and Revett were engraved. The drawings for *Palmyra* and *Baalbec* were made by an architect named Boura, presumably from his sketches made on the spot. They are timidly drawn in line and wash, and as the geometrical drawings show the buildings not as they were, but as restored, their archæological value is small. Stuart's original drawings were badly drawn and heavily laboured in body colour, but in the very skilful hands of old Rooker, who engraved the plates for the first volume, which appeared in 1762, these absurd draw-

---

* The reader will find these folios discussed at greater length in Vol. II., Chap. XIII., of my *History of Renaissance Architecture in England*.

Section of Kedleston. By J. Gandon. From *Vitruvius Britannicus* (Vol. IV.)

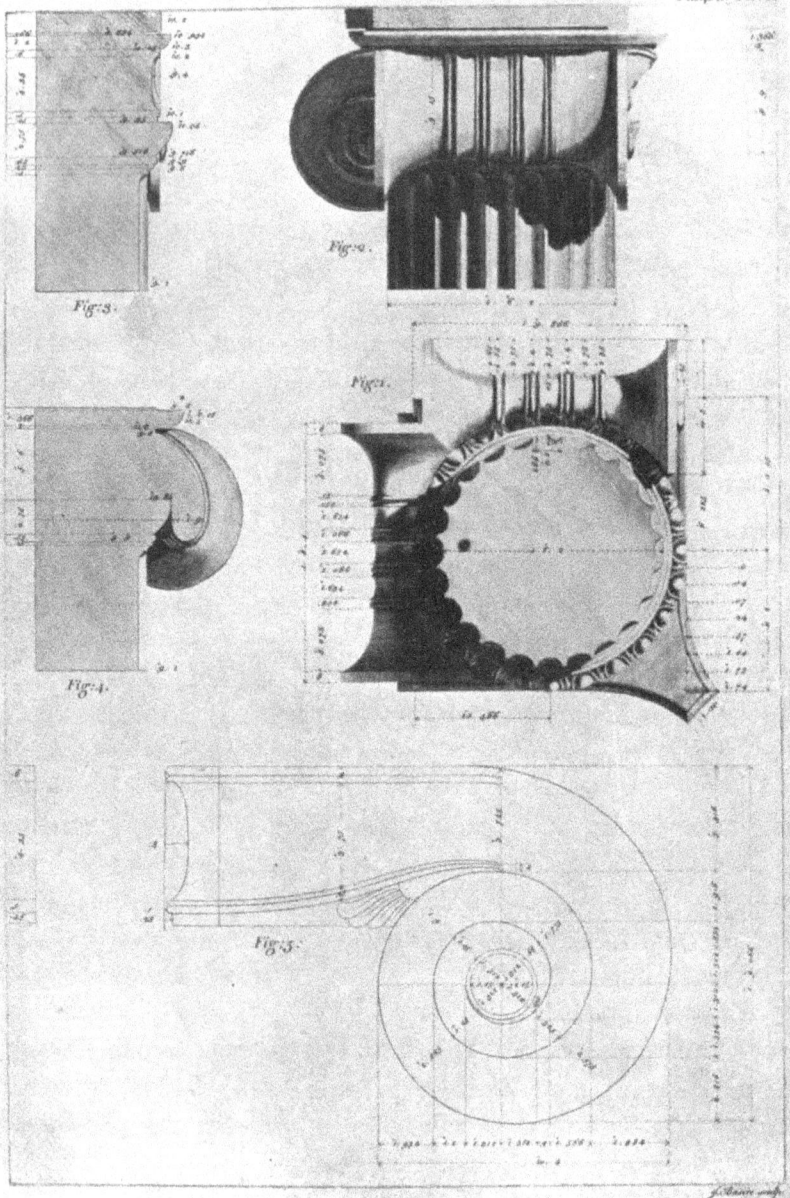

Ionic Capital. Engraved by James Basire. From Stuart and Revett's
Athenian Antiquities

ings became quite respectable. William Inwood, who visited Athens in 1818, made some much better drawings of the Acropolis, now at South Kensington. The scholarly labours of Cockerell and Penrose carried on this tradition, and in recent years excellent work has been done, though it has rather unfortunately drifted away from architecture into archæology. From the draughtsman's point of view, however, there is not much to be learnt from this work, depending as it does on scientific accuracy of drawing rather than on those qualities of selection and suggestiveness in treatment which are the special study of the draughtsman, in so far as his problem is the interpretation and rendering of ideas rather than the mechanical statement of facts.

We must now retrace our steps and pick up the threads of that tradition of topographical draughtsmanship which, in England, dates from the latter part of the seventeenth century. From the Restoration to the Revolution of 1688 the relations of the French and English Courts were friendly, and engravings by French artists were on sale in the London print shops in the Strand.* These, no doubt, stimulated the fashion for topographical drawings. Most of the drawings by Jean Marot and the Perelle, illustrating the great French houses, had appeared in France before 1688, and must have been known in England. The worst of it was that there were no English draughtsmen available as yet. Prior to the Revocation of the Edict of Nantes, Frenchmen were too well employed in France to find it worth their while to settle in England. English art was still isolated. The days of the " Grand Tour " were only just beginning, and Italy had not yet recovered much of the vast popularity it was to enjoy in the eighteenth

* I have found on two prints of Lepautre the name of an English printseller : " Printed and sold by Saml. Sympson, at his house in Catherine Street, Strand, where is sold a great variety of Italian, French, and Dutch prints."

82 Architectural Drawing and Draughtsmen

century. The result was that we had to fall back on the industrious German and Dutchman.

David Loggan, a precise and excellent draughtsman, who brought out his *Oxonia Illustrata* in 1675, followed by *Cantabrigia Illustrata* in 1688, was a native of Dantzig. Michael Burghers, who did a good deal of work in illustration of country houses, was a Dutchman, who settled at Oxford, and engraved the headpieces of the Oxford almanacs for many years after 1676. Kip and Knyff, who made all the plates in the *Britannia Illustrata*, were Dutchmen, and between them they produced a very interesting and successful book. The first volume, containing eighty plates, appeared in 1709.* A second volume, containing sixty more, appeared in 1717; and in a republication of the two volumes a note appeared, announcing that "there is a third volume in hand, any gentleman paying five guineas towards the graving may have their seat inserted, it being very forward, which is only half what the former paid." The engravings, which are nearly all bird's-eye views, are considerably larger than Perelle's, and not nearly so good : Kip and Knyff had a way of putting their horizontal line above the top of the picture and then forgetting to run their vanishing lines out, so that the line of horizon appears to be the edge of a cliff dropping abruptly into space.

The taste for topographical draughtsmanship was well established in England early in the eighteenth century, but two fresh factors were now to come into play—the Grand Tour and the romantic movement, that curious hankering after the mysterious

---

* Roget (*History of the Old Water-Colour Society*) says : " The first volume, containing eighty plates, appeared in 1714." My own copy, however, is dated 1709. I am greatly indebted to Mr. Roget's excellent work for an account of the earlier English draughtsmen. I do not follow him, however, when he says that Kip and Knyff used three separate horizon lines. As far as I can make out, they used one above the picture, but forgot to let their lines vanish out. Many of the views were reproduced on a tiny scale in that delightful little guide-book, *Les Délices de la Grande-Bretagne*.

and abnormal, and that sentimental affection for ruin and decay which began to assert themselves when classicism was in full sway and apparently enjoying an assured predominance. It appears, as I have already pointed out, in a most remarkable form in Piranesi's etchings and engravings, and it inspired, at a much lower level, Hubert Robert's facile compositions of ruins, which had a prodigious vogue in France before the French Revolution. In England its effects were more conspicuous in literature than in art. But towards the middle of the eighteenth century, ruins and romantic landscapes were coming into favour, and medieval architecture began to attract enthusiastic if uncritical curiosity.

Towards the latter part of the seventeenth century France became to all intents a closed country to Englishmen. Moreover, the supremacy of France in the arts had never been admitted in England. Burlington was the apostle of Palladio. The admirable manner of Wren, that delightful blend of English good sense and French accomplishment, was condemned as unscholarly. The Grand Tour was indispensable to any young nobleman who aspired to being considered a connoisseur, and the Grand Tour meant Italy, the old masters, and those clever artists of the eighteenth century who industriously cultivated this lucrative market for their interminable views of the ruins of Roman architecture. Canaletto dedicated his book of views*￼to Joseph Smith, his Majesty's Consul at Venice "*in segno di stimio ed ossequio.*" Piranesi's relations with Lord Charlemont I have already referred to, and Piranesi was a Fellow of the Society of Antiquaries. In Italy the taste for ruins (the ruins of Rome and Italy, whether real or imaginary made little difference) was universal and inveterate, and all who had qualified by the Grand Tour returned to England steeped in this extraordinary

---

* *Vedute altre prese da i Luoghi, altre ideale, da Antonio Canaletto.* On one of the drawings is a date, 1741.

taste, a taste indeed that was not less popular in France than it was in Italy and England. Diderot, most readable of critics, writing of the Salon of 1767, and referring to Robert's reception picture at the Academy of the " Port de Rome," went so far as to say that a palace only became interesting when it was ruined. Of architecture, its aims and possible merits, he was blandly unconscious. The " ideal " was all in all, but the " ideal " to Diderot was not the ideal of the art, but the sentiment with which the fancy of some literary man happened to invest the subject of his choice. Here is the passage in full : *" Il y a plus de poésie, plus d'accidents, je ne dis pas dans un chaumière, mais dans un seul arbre qui a souffert des années et des saisons, que dans toute la façade d'un palais. Il faut ruiner un palais pour en faire un objet d'intérêt. Tant il est vrai que point de beauté vraie sans l'idéal."* This is not John Ruskin writing in 1867, but Denis Diderot, the encyclopædist a hundred years before ; but the touch is the same and the kinship obvious, perhaps the only difference being that Diderot knew quite well what he was doing when he used the familiar weapons of the rhetorician—the paradox, the popular appeal, the acrobatic thought, the confusion of premises, and the half-truth or no truth.

Robert, a facile and clever draughtsman, bad at the figure and inaccurate in perspective, was quick to profit by the encouragement of such men as Diderot and Rousseau, and did a prosperous trade in ruins and perspectives down to the days of the French Revolution, when all this playing with ruins and nature was swept into space.

Meanwhile, things had been moving on more or less parallel lines in England, but with results quite different. The age of Addison was over ; the comfortable assurance that everything was for the best as it was, was giving way to a fancy, half sincere, half sentimental, that everything had been very much better in the

Italian Garden Scene. From a Drawing possibly by Hubert Robert in the Collection of the Royal
Institute of British Architects

Eton College. By Paul Sandby. From the Drawing in the British Museum

Middle Ages. Richard Hurd, Bishop of Worcester, a competent scholar and critic, trained in the strictest sects of the classicists, is found in 1762 defending Gothic architecture, urging that it has its own rules of practice and canons of design as much as classic. It is true that this argument was only an incident in his defence of Tasso and Spenser. Writing with the airy indifference to facts of the literary man of the eighteenth century, Hurd says: " This Gothic method of design in poetry may be in some sort illustrated by what is called the Gothic method of design in gardening." But he then proceeds to describe, not the " *hortus inclusus*," which was, in fact, the garden of the Middle Ages, but the method of laying out grounds in avenues, which was borrowed by English designers from Le Notre, and was surely " classical " in the sense that it was regular, symmetrical, and observant of unity of idea. Hurd's defence of Gothic was not more genuine than the efforts of Pope and Horace Walpole a generation before, but Hurd's influence did a good deal to consolidate the romantic movement, and the consequence was that, whereas Italian and French artists turned out interminable presentations of classical ruins, the taste in England was all for the Gothic. The ruined castle and the dismantled abbey replaced the arches of the Colosseum. Draughtsmen were busy everywhere, drawing the remains of Gothic architecture. The vagaries of the literary man had resulted in a most unfortunate division of views as to the meaning and purpose of architecture. On the one hand there was the solid classic of the eighteenth century, still being practised by very able men such as Ware, Chambers, Carr of York, Paine, and the Adams. On the other hand, there was this amateur theory of Gothic architecture, a theory based on sentiment and not on historical knowledge or critical study. The amateurs, on the strong current of the romantic movement, carried the day, and have retarded the development of architecture in the country by at least a hundred years; and though it is useless to attempt to put back the clock, one cannot but regret the disastrous extent to which the cleavage between classic and romantic art was driven home. For the romance was not genuine romance; it was not the expression of an age of great adventure, such as had inspired the Elizabethans, but the faded fancy of literary sentimentalists, and its only contributions to the arts of Europe have been landscape gardening and the Gothic revival.

Architectural draughtsmanship followed the fashion. The architects continued to publish their folios, but the demand for them was dwindling, and artists and draughtsmen found more profitable employment in making picturesque views of buildings, and romantic landscapes.*

The Sandbys were typical of this period. The two brothers were born at Nottingham. Thomas, the elder, who had begun his career as draughtsman to the chief engineer at Fort William, and was present at Culloden, was made a member of the Royal Academy at its foundation in 1768, and was its first professor of architecture. Paul Sandby, who also began as an engineer's draughtsman, was employed on a survey of the North-West Highlands, and while so employed made a series of landscape drawings which he published as etchings. He also was an original member of the Royal Academy, enjoyed the patronage of some very wealthy and distinguished gentlemen, and was made deputy ranger of the Great Park at Windsor under the Duke of Cumberland. He was much in the fashion, and is said to have been the first English artist to work in aquatint, but he was a moderate draughtsman and a most inferior painter. The view of Eton College in the British Museum which I reproduce shows him at his best, and the most interesting work

---

* See Roget, *History of the Old Water-Colour Society*, for an excellent account of such publications as the works of Samuel and Nathaniel Buck, Malton, Watts, Angus, Thomas Hearne, John Carter, and the elder Pugin.

ST GEORGES, HANOVER SQUARE.

St. George's, Hanover Square. By Thomas Malton. In the Soane Museum

View of Dance's Design for the Improvement of the Port of London. Drawn and Engraved by William Daniel (1802)

of his that I know is the dining-room at Drakelowe (Sir Robert Gresley), entirely covered with painting in tempera of the scenery of Derbyshire. The idea was to give the illusion of being in the open air. Instead of a dado, a park fence in trellis is fixed to the face of the wall, and the landscape starts from this, and is carried up the wall, over a cove, and into the sky (the ceiling) without any break whatever. It is a very curious example of the taste of the time, skilfully executed as a matter of scene-painting, but wholly destitute of any sense of architecture. The chimney-piece, built in Derbyshire spar, was apparently intended to suggest a hole in the rocks. Thomas Sandby was the better man of the two, and at one time seems to have had a faint ambition to follow the lead of Bibiena and the Italians. There is a drawing by him which suggests a far-off echo of the manner of those skilful artists, but the fashion was too strong for him, and he drifted off into a lucrative practice of view-making.

The Sandbys were not considerable artists. Thomas Malton,* who had served three years in Gandon's office, and taught Turner perspective, was a much better architectural draughtsman; and some of those coloured prints of London buildings published by Ackermann—for instance, the plate of St. George's, Hanover Square—show more accomplishment and sense of architecture than was possessed by either of the Sandbys. Within their comparatively narrow limits of technique, some of these plates are models of tinted drawings of architecture. The colouring is just sufficient for its purpose, often controlled by a delicate sense of values, and the draughtsmanship and perspective are accurate and precise. Ackermann got hold of some very good men, and it is unfortunate that

---

* Malton was born in 1748, and exhibited constantly in the Royal Academy between 1768 and 1803. He gave lessons in drawing in Conduit Street, and among other things painted scenery for Covent Garden. A list of his works is given by Roget (*History of the Old Water-Colour Society*).

the lead in architectural drawing set by these excellent views was quite forgotten in the middle and latter part of the nineteenth century. I give a remarkable print, drawn and engraved by William Daniel,* 1802, to illustrate the younger Dance's design for the improvement of the Port of London.

The Sandbys are only important as forerunners of the great English school of water-colour, through Cotman and Dayes, to Turner, Varley, and Girtin, that incomparable master whose early death was an irreparable loss to English art. The aquatints of Paris, in which Girtin was engaged almost up to the day of his death,† are models of what drawings in line and wash should be, in their breadth and simplicity of statement, solid composition, and wonderful suggestion of atmosphere and the environment of buildings. That fine artist, J. S. Cotman, shows something of this faculty in the drawing of Dieppe at South Kensington (3013. 76), and its entire absence is to be noted in Prout's heavy and insensitive water colours. I believe if Prout had drawn the Parthenon he would have given it the quality of St. Pierre at Caen, and presented it with the atmosphere of Ratisbon or Würzburg.

In the early part of the last century, and indeed before, architecture as a subject played a large part in English water-colour painting, and it was inevitable that the original intention of the representation of architecture should be lost sight of, and that buildings should come to be treated merely as an element of composition without regard to accuracy of statement. The worst qualities of the romantic movement, its sentimentalism, its loose-

* William Daniel, nephew of Thomas Daniel, and author with him of *Oriental Scenery*, was elected an Associate of the Royal Academy in 1807, and Academician in 1822. He died in 1857. The draughtsmanship shown in the views of the Port of London is finer than anything in the *Oriental Scenery*.

† The Peace of Amiens (October 1st, 1801) reopened France to Englishmen. Girtin, who was very ill, went to Paris in the hope of recovery, and made the drawings from his carriage ; but his condition became worse, and he died in his studio in the autumn following, at the age of twenty-seven.

Nôtre Dame, Paris. By Thomas Girtin. Collection of W. C. Alexander, Esq.

Porte St. Denis, Paris. By Thomas Girtin

Dieppe. By John Sell Cotman. In the South Kensington Museum

The Tower, Laon Cathedral. By W. E. Nesfield. In the Collection of the
Royal Institute of British Architects

ness of thought and expression, took firm hold of the painters, and appear in the vague architecture of Turner, most splendid, yet in a way most retrograde, of painters. Unfortunately, the rift had opened between the painter and the draughtsman of architecture, a rift that steadily widened through the last century, and is only now beginning to close up again, as painters have begun to realise something of the fascination of architecture, and architects have tired of being isolated in the Arts. Early in the last century technical architectural draughtsmanship seems to have been cut off in a backwater. It ceased to be regarded as art, and those who practised it gradually evolved a system of conventions which deprived their drawings of any value, except such as could be derived from the setting up of a building in perspective, presumably accurate in scale.

The habit of outline drawing of architecture, introduced by the elder Pugin, has much to answer for. It has taught architectural students to look at buildings not as masses, as compositions of solids and voids, but as arrangements of abstract lines; and it has withdrawn their attention from that study of form in the round which is the province of the architect not less than of the sculptor. There is no necessity to dwell on the aberrations of the professional architectural draughtsman of the 'sixties. He is now nearly extinct, and his work was a failure, because it relied on tricks and conventions and not on genuine drawing, and because he conceived of his problem as mechanical and not as one that called for thought and the play of imagination. It has, however, been overlooked by artists that among the architects of the last century there were some very able draughtsmen. Gandy, who made a number of drawings for Sir John Soane, was an artist of exceptional ability. Blore drew his Gothic detail very well, and both the Cockerells were accomplished draughtsmen. George Devey had a wonderful knack of turning out picturesque projects of buildings. Nesfield, though

M

he never wholly recovered from the unfortunate influence of J. D. Harding, became a consummate draughtsman of architecture. His drawings of French cathedrals are infinitely finer than those cast-iron drawings by Viollet le Duc, some of which Ruskin very properly described as " beastly." Burges could have drawn anything he liked, if only he could have forgotten that he was a medievalist. Street was a rapid and skilful draughtsman ; Waterhouse a master of large competition perspectives, such as the one I illustrate ; and the clean draughtsmanship shown in the volume that Mr. Shaw published in 1858, and in his Academy drawings for many years, is still in its way a model for students.

With this one exception I do not deal with living artists, with those among us who have done much to rescue the art from the rut into which it had fallen, and to maintain that tradition of architectural scholarship in which England was once supreme. Moreover, artists not especially trained in architecture have shown what fine material for their art is to be found in noble buildings. The level has been raised all round, and in quite recent years draughtsmanship has made a notable advance in this country and America, under the inspiration of that high standard of drawing which is the greatest tradition of the École des Beaux-Arts. The result is that architectural draughtsmanship now stands in a very different position from what it did thirty years ago. But danger still lurks in the background, and the danger is that students, instead of learning to become good draughtsmen—that is, instead of acquiring the power of drawing anything by study of buildings, of natural objects, and of the life—tend to concentrate on the fashionable manner of the time. At present it is the French manner—excellent, accomplished, and within narrow limits perfectly adequate ; but it has been my object in these essays to show that the modern French manner is only one among many others, a manner too, which, though it expresses the habit of mind

Chartres Cathedral. By W. E. Nesfield. In the Collection of the Royal
Institute of British Architects

Competition Drawing of Design for the Law Courts. By the late Alfred Waterhouse, R.A. In the Collection of the Royal Institute of British Architects

of French designers, does not necessarily respond to the difference of temperament and tradition of the Anglo-Saxon. Before the student succumbs to this or to any other convention, he should study widely, he should acquaint himself with what has been done by great masters in the past—Bramante, the younger San Gallo, Peruzzi, the Marot, Perelle and Lepautre, Piranesi, and our own English masters of draughtsmanship. And, before all, he should draw for himself. It is a mistake to suppose that architectural drawing is cut off from the world of art. Even our geometrical drawings are something more than the scientific diagrams of the engineer, and I have already called attention to the fact that blundering and incompetence here nearly always means failure in the executed work. The fine drawing of architecture is like the fine drawing of anything else, except that the specialised knowledge in this case is the knowledge and understanding of architectural forms. So far as art is concerned there is no essential difference between the drawing of a building and the drawing of a figure. We do not accept, nowadays, symbols and conventions of figures. We must be shown the actual object, the scheme and symmetry of the whole, the shaping and modelling of the parts. So it is with architecture. Merely mechanical diagrams are not enough, and mere virtuosity of drawing, tricks of line, or of black and white, are no use to us. What we want is the thing itself, in the largest sense of the phrase, and the only draughtsmanship which will live is that which is sincere in purpose, loyal and faithful in execution. A modern critic* has somewhere spoken of certain draughtsmanship as "caressing." That quality, rightly understood, is the quality of all fine drawing : the frankness and candour of the open mind, the close observation of the eye sensitive to every nuance of outline and modelling, the assured freedom of hand and lightness of touch that can transmit the impression undimmed by inadequate technique.

* Sir Sidney Colvin.

INDEX

Index

95